Breaking the Sout

Breaking the
South Slav Dream

The Rise and Fall of Yugoslavia

KATE HUDSON

Pluto Press

LONDON • STERLING, VIRGINIA

First published 2003 by Pluto Press
345 Archway Road, London N6 5AA
and 22883 Quicksilver Drive,
Sterling, VA 20166–2012, USA

www.plutobooks.com

British Library Cataloguing in Publication Data
A catalogue record for this book is available from the British Library

ISBN 0 7453 1882 7 hardback
ISBN 0 7453 1881 9 paperback

Library of Congress Cataloging in Publication Data
Hudson, Kate, 1958–
   Breaking the South Slav dream : the rise and fall of Yugoslavia / Kate
Hudson.
     p. cm.
   ISBN 0–7453–1882–7
   1. Yugoslavia—History. I. Title.
   DR1246 .H83 2003
   949.702—dc21
                                                        2003004680

10   9   8   7   6   5   4   3   2   1

Designed and produced for Pluto Press by
Chase Publishing Services, Fortescue, Sidmouth EX10 9QG, England
Typeset from disk by Stanford DTP Services, Towcester, England
Printed and bound in the European Union by
Antony Rowe Ltd, Chippenham, Wiltshire, England

Contents

For my mother, Moira Hudson, with love and thanks.

Introduction

Little more than a decade ago, Yugoslavia – the south slav state – symbolized a progressive and open socialist society, held in high regard internationally for its monumental struggles for unity and independence and its role as a key leader of the Non-Aligned Movement. In the last decade, however, assisted by an intense campaign in the western media, Yugoslavia has instead become a byword for a kind of primordial 'ethnic' hatred and conflict, whereby previously peaceful communities inexplicably descended into frenzies of killing and atrocities, and subsequently required the good offices of the 'civilized' west to keep them apart, show them how to run their 'emerging democracies' and insert them into the global market economy. This seemingly inexplicable degener-ation is, however, more readily understandable in the context of western aims and strategic interests in eastern Europe. These aims have at times worked in Yugoslavia's favour – through, for example, US, British and French support for the establishment of the state after the First World War as a bulwark against German expansion-ism and Soviet Russia – and at times against – since, for example, the collapse of communism in 1989, the break-up of Yugoslavia into easily-dominated pieces, and the incorporation of the region into the economic and military framework of western institutions.

It is not the intention to suggest that the relationship between the western powers and Yugoslavia has been a one-way street of western hostility – rather that their attitudes towards Yugoslavia have varied according to their strategic aims and it is these which have primarily, although not exclusively, determined Yugoslavia's trajectory. It is notable and clarificatory that Yugoslavia's key period of peaceful development was when it was shielded from conflict-ing goals by its special relationship with the west following Yugoslavia's split with the Soviet Union in the late 1940s. It served the purposes of the west at that time to have a stable, united and neutral Yugoslavia, but once the threat of the Soviet Union had been removed there was no longer any need for the west to help maintain a non-aligned socialist country between NATO and the Warsaw Pact, and such favoured status disappeared. Indeed, it was the United States that took the lead in destroying Yugoslavia's socialist economy, although initially it did not support the break-up of the Federation. It hoped instead that a unified, free-market economy Yugoslavia could be developed under the leadership of Ante Markovic. Notwithstanding US intentions at this point, however, it was primarily the disastrous economic problems caused by the IMF policies imposed on Yugoslavia in the 1980s which provoked the crisis that eventually resulted in the break-up of the federal republic.

This process was encouraged by Germany's recognition of the secessionist republics of Slovenia and Croatia as it sought to Balkanize the region and re-extend its inter-war hegemony in eastern Europe. The US's precipitate recognition of Bosnia – against the advice of its own experts – resulted not only in a terrible war, but also in the US firmly establishing a presence in the region. This process was taken one stage further by the NATO assault on Yugoslavia in 1999 and the subsequent establishment of what is effectively a NATO protectorate in Kosovo. The NATO bombardment of Kosovo did not succeed, however, in achieving what had become the key aim of the US and EU: the removal from power of the Yugoslav leader, Slobodan Milosevic, who was resisting full free-market reform and integration into western institutions. This goal was finally achieved in 2000, when Milosevic was defeated in a presidential election which had been the target of unprecedented western intervention. In 2003, the component republics of Yugoslavia voted to replace the Federal Republic of Yugoslavia with the Union of Serbia and Montenegro.

The south slav dream of a united, viable state, which would enable them to resist Balkanization by western economic and geo-strategic interests and determine their own destiny and development, was finally broken.

The reasons for the break-up of Yugoslavia remain much debated, as do the proportions of blame that are to be allocated for the brutal nature of the wars that accompanied that process. In western governmental circles, two views can be identified. The first was that the break-up resulted from a pattern of Serbian aggression, from Slovenia and Croatia through to Bosnia-Hercegovina, with the purpose of creating a Greater Serbia. This perspective, according to Susan Woodward, originated amongst the leaders of Austria,

Slovenia, Croatia and subsequently Germany. It was then taken up by the US government, which used it 'for the identification of a more general pattern in the post-cold war period of what American officials called rogue or renegade states, headed by "new Hitlers" such as Saddam Hussein in Iraq and Slobodan Milosevic, who defied all norms of civilised behavior and had to be punished to protect those norms and to protect innocent people.'[1]

The second perspective was that the Yugoslav conflict 'constituted a civil war based on the revival of ethnic conflict after the fall of communism'.[2] This view, which was more popular in Europe and Canada – although it did have some support in the US – saw the events in Yugoslavia during the 1990s as history reasserting itself once the lid of communist suppression had been lifted. That history was perceived to have been one of ethnic hostility and conflict. The erroneous nature of both of these views will be demonstrated in the course of this book.

A range of scholarly writings also exists, dealing both with specific aspects of the subject and with the wider issues. David Chandler has written on Bosnia[3] since the Dayton Accords, and Noel Malcolm has written short histories of both Bosnia[4] and Kosovo.[5] Susan Woodward's *Balkan Tragedy*,[6] published in 1995, draws a broader picture of the early years of the conflict but there are some weaknesses in her analysis. Her explanation of the conflict as residing in the disintegration of governmental authority in Yugoslavia and a more widespread phenomenon of political disintegration, does not get to the heart of the matter – external interests in the region and the obstacle that a unified, and particularly socialist, Yugoslavia ultimately presented to those interests. Other recent works that have attempted to give an overarching assessment of the issues are John B. Allcock's *Explaining Yugoslavia*[7] and Misha Glenny's *The Balkans*.[8] These works ask the right questions but reach the wrong conclusions. Allcock emphasizes economic factors in explaining Yugoslavia but in too narrow a context. He suggests, for example, that factors such as the 1974 constitution or the 1976 labour law contributed as much as anything else to Yugoslavia's demise, which is to overemphasize their significance considerably and to diminish the wider factors. Glenny argues correctly that ethnic violence is a consequence rather than a cause of Balkan instability, which is itself primarily the result of external interference, but he argues incorrectly that the tolerance in the region, in earlier times, was destroyed by the arrival of European nationalist ideas in the nineteenth century. This book argues rather, that such ideas contributed to the liberation of the region from the great powers, which have subsequently, when it suited them, frustrated attempts at genuine independence within the region.

Chapter 1 looks at the origins of Yugoslavia in the aspirations of the south slav peoples in the nineteenth century, the necessity of its formation as an antidote to 'Balkanization', and the struggles for self-determination which resulted in the achievement of that goal in 1919. Serbia's leading role in achieving unity and liberation for the south slav peoples and the support of the component parts for Serbia in that role is considered, as is the preponderance which the pre-unification Serbian state eventually achieved in the new Yugoslavia. The motives of the victorious powers for supporting the creation of Yugoslavia – as a buffer against a resurgent Germany and a revolutionary Russia – are also analysed. The economic and political problems of the inter-war years are outlined, including the impact of the economic crash of 1929. During the 1930s Yugoslavia became increasingly economically dependent on Germany, but her failure to comply with the political requirements of Nazi Germany led to invasion and dismemberment in 1941.

Chapter 2 covers the period of the Second World War, the Balkanization and occupation of Yugoslavia by enemy forces and its eventual reunification under the leadership of the communist resistance leader, Josip Broz Tito. It is argued that occupied Yugoslavia was the site of struggle not only for national liberation but also for the nature of the post-war political, social and economic order. The military and political forces of the pre-war monarchy were discredited and defeated – not least because of their military collaboration with the occupying forces. The communist partisan movement with its all-Yugoslav principles, its undoubted bravery and its social egalitarianism won overwhelming popular support and emerged from the devastation of the war to form a new, united, federal state.

Chapter 3 looks at the stabilization of the country in the post-war period and its position, after the rift with Moscow, as a communist country balancing between east and west. The US sought to widen this division in the Soviet bloc by supplying Yugoslavia with economic aid, but Tito never joined the NATO camp and it is argued that he exploited Cold War antagonisms to sustain political independence from Moscow and the west while constructing a socialist-oriented society at home. With the collapse of communism in eastern Europe in 1989, the US was no longer interested in backing a communist Yugoslavia and turned towards its marketization and the break-up of the complex system of economic and social self-management which was the hallmark of Yugoslav socialism. This was a significant factor in its ultimate political and territorial dismemberment.

Chapter 4 explains how, from 1984, US policy favoured increased efforts to overthrow communism and reintroduce capitalism into eastern Europe. Yugoslavia's growing indebtedness to western institutions gave the latter considerable leverage over the Yugoslav economy and the introduction of IMF-sponsored, liberal macroeconomic reform led to austerity and deterioration in living standards. Economic collapse fuelled increasing tension and eventual conflict between the republics as the wealthier republics like Slovenia and Croatia were encouraged to hope for greater prosperity within the German economic zone. The economic crisis also exacerbated tensions within Serbia over the constitutional status of the autonomous provinces, most notably that of Kosovo.

Chapter 5 considers the response of the different federal republics to the economic crisis of the 1980s. The political leaderships in Slovenia and Croatia backed the deepening of free-market forces but did not support the centralizing tendencies of the IMF reforms. They began to pursue secession from the federation. In Serbia there was simultaneously huge popular opposition to the liberal market policies of the federal government, and a positive attitude towards the recentralizing policies of the IMF. Multi-party elections took place in the republics in 1990, with nationalist parties coming to power in Slovenia and Croatia where independence was declared in 1991. Serbia and Montenegro elected communist or former communist parties and declared their determination to remain within a federal republic of Yugoslavia.

Chapter 6 charts the first phase of the war in the 1990s – in Croatia. While the secession of Slovenia was relatively bloodless, thousands died in the war in Croatia, for which, it is argued, foreign governments must bear considerable responsibility for encouraging secessionism. Foreign backing of separatists militated against a negotiated settlement and Germany was particularly implicated in this. The catalyst for the war was Croatia's new constitution, which stripped the Serbs in Croatia of many of their rights, refusing to accept their right to self-determination which had existed under the Yugoslav constitution. The Serbs in Croatia fought to remain within Yugoslavia and were eventually supported by the Yugoslav army in that goal.

Chapter 7 notes the responsibility of the US for the second wave of war – in Bosnia-Hercegovina. Recognition of Bosnian independence, in the political and strategic interests of the US and without the agreement of all constituent nationalities as required by the constitution, led to war. The Serbian community did not wish to leave Yugoslavia and fought to control Serb-occupied lands, declaring the Serbian Republic of Bosnia-Hercegovina. It is observed that a systematic media campaign vilified the Serbs as genocidal aggressors, whereas international agencies have noted that atrocities were committed on all sides and Serbs were on occasion framed for controversial atrocities for which they were not responsible. The war was concluded after the NATO bombardment of the Bosnian Serbs and was followed by the establishment of an international protectorate in Bosnia.

Chapter 8 outlines the third wave of war in Kosovo. It is argued that the legitimate grievances of the Kosovan Albanians were manipulated by the west and used to justify the attempts to destroy the remaining parts of the socialist economy of Yugoslavia and open the region fully to liberal market economics. The war was portrayed as a conflict between Serbs and Albanians with the west conducting a humanitarian intervention on behalf of the latter to secure their safety and self-determination against the Serb aggressors. It is here acknowledged that extremist elements in the Kosovan Albanian community provoked the Yugoslav forces in order to justify NATO intervention and secure Kosovan independence and that they won support from the US in order to bring about the overthrow of Milosevic. On conclusion of the war, however, Milosevic remained in power, and Kosovo – rather than achieving self-determination – became a UN/NATO protectorate.

Chapter 9 looks at the defeat of Milosevic in the presidential election in September 2000 and the role of external forces in the election process. The US in particular played a substantial role in the provision of funding, training and advice for the opposition forces in Serbia. It is argued that Milosevic had a solid base of genuine support amongst the population and it was inaccurate to describe him as a dictator. However, the weight of military, economic and political intervention in the election – rendering it far from fair and democratic – ensured that he would be defeated. Following the election, conflict emerged between the moderate nationalist President Kostunica and the strongly pro-western prime minister Djindjic who promoted rapid liberal economic reform prior to his assassination in March 2003. On 4 February 2003, the Yugoslav parliament approved the Constitutional Charter of the new state of Serbia and Montenegro.

Chapter 10 reviews the trial of Slobodan Milosevic which opened at the Hague in February 2002. Milosevic is accused of 66 charges of war crimes arising from the wars in Croatia, Bosnia and Kosovo. Milosevic regards the trial as a politically motivated attack to justify the crimes committed against Yugoslavia. The charges are based on the principle that Milosevic, as president of Yugoslavia, had command responsibility for crimes committed by institutions and forces answerable to him. Milosevic argues that a number of the charges are false, being wilful misrepresentations of events for political reasons – such as the alleged massacre at Racak, and that others he had no knowledge of, actively sought to prevent, or appropriately punished those responsible for criminal behaviour. It is noted that the prosecution has, so far, been unsuccessful in making a convincing case for Milosevic's complicity in war crimes.

1
The 'first' Yugoslavia: origins and problems

Yugoslavia, in the geographic form that it was known during its seven decades of existence, was created out of the ruins of two of the great territorial empires of central and eastern Europe at the end of the First World War. The creation of the Yugoslav state was an aspiration of the south slav peoples, first manifested and articulated in the nineteenth century, and decades of struggle for self-determination ensued before the goal was finally achieved. The Paris Peace Conference of 1919, which laid to rest the Austro-Hungarian, German and Ottoman Empires, recognized and allowed the establishment of the state of Yugoslavia, together with those of Poland, Hungary, Bulgaria, Romania, Czechoslovakia and Albania.

The desire for the formation of Yugoslavia emerged out of the realization that only a unified south slav state could be viable in the face of competing regional economic and strategic interests. Indeed, Yugoslavia was the only possible antidote to 'Balkanization' – the division of the area into small antagonistic states, which would have no hope of real independence and self-determination. Serbia led the formation of this state – as was indeed desired by the other component parts prior to their liberation – because Serbia was the largest south slav community around which the other communities could cohere. It had already liberated itself from Ottoman rule and established a nation state, and was struggling to liberate other south slav peoples prior to the First World War.

The collapse of the Austro-Hungarian and Ottoman Empires made the longed-for unification achievable and – fortunately for the south slavs – the situation at the end of the war made it desirable for the Great Powers that such a state should exist. While the nation states of central and eastern Europe were ostensibly founded on the Wilsonian principles of national self-determination – named after US President Wilson who championed such principles as a way of weakening the British and French Empires – in fact, wider political and strategic issues were at stake. The containment of

Germany, which would urgently seek to revise the conditions of the post-war peace treaty, was of crucial importance. A resurgent Germany was inevitable; therefore the stronger the west's allies to its east, the better. A unified south slav state, led by the Serbs who were war-time allies of Britain, France and the US, and implacably hostile to Germany, was a very positive option for the great powers. Furthermore, a viable state under strong leadership could help to defuse or suppress radical tendencies among peasants and workers in the aftermath of the Russian Revolution and the devastation wrought by the First World War. Yugoslavia under Serbian leadership could also help bring this type of stability to the region.

The new state of Yugoslavia was complex and diverse, histori-cally, politically and culturally, as were many of the new states of central and eastern Europe. During the inter-war period it faced a three-fold challenge: to maintain its independence and territorial integrity in the face of revisionist claims by the powers defeated in the First World War; to resolve the national question within Yugoslavia thus ensuring the stability of the new state; and to resolve the social questions and ensure the equality and prosperity of the population as a whole. While the new Yugoslav state provided the framework within which all these problems could be resolved, none of them, in fact, were. Economic weakness and diplomatic isolation in the context of the strengthening fascist powers meant that Yugoslavia was vulnerable to German economic and strategic interests. The failure of the centralized state to allow a federal system and ensure equality of the constituent peoples led to dissatisfaction, particularly from the Croatian elites. Insufficient investment in agriculture, in the context of the economic crash of 1929, led to great hardship for the primarily rural population. Thus, when Yugoslavia was broken up by the Axis powers in 1941, the prognosis was not good for the south slav state. A second oppor-tunity to resolve these issues was eventually provided under the leadership of the Communist Party of Yugoslavia: the only pan-Yugoslav political organization, committed to a federal Yugoslavia organized on the basis of social and economic equality.

YUGOSLAVISM AND THE ORIGINS OF THE STATE

As Joseph Rothschild has observed, it was the First World War that 'permitted the political realization of that "Yugoslav dream" whose ideological roots lay in nineteenth-century romanticism and nationalism'.[1] Its material roots, of course, lay in the fact that it was only through banding together that the south slavs could be independent, and it was primarily from the Croats of the Austro-Hungarian Empire, who sought independence from Hapsburg rule, that this dream emerged in the mid-nineteenth century. The Croatian national revival had come about partly as a response to Hungarian nationalism within the Austrian Empire in the late eighteenth century. The Hungarian nobility replaced Latin-language usage with Hungarian and subsequently the Croats built their own language-based national movement – the Illyrian movement of the 1830s and 1840s. The orientation of the Illyrian movement – named after the ancient Illyrians who were believed to have been the ancestors of the south slavs – was towards a south slav culture and consciousness. The movement was crushed, however, after the defeat of the 1848 revolutions across Europe, and for a number of years a more straightforward Croatian nation-alism dominated the political agenda, as well as what appeared to be a more realizable aspiration of establishing greater Croatian independence within a federal Austria-Hungary. However, it was the Croatian intelligentsia which again gave rise to the Yugoslav idea. As Mihailo Crnobrnja has pointed out: 'The principal proponent of Yugoslavism was Bishop Josip Strossmayer, who, in establishing the Yugoslav Academy of Sciences in Zagreb in 1866, created the first institution ever to bear the Yugoslav name.'[2] Strossmayer's vision was for a federal south slav state, uniting the slavs of the Austro-Hungarian Empire with Montenegro and Serbia. In the early years of the twentieth century, the first Croat and Serb political party – the Serb-Croat Coalition – was founded and rapidly won a large majority in the Croatian parliament, based on the idea of Croat and Serb national unity. Crnobrnja describes this as 'the most important political idea in pre-war Croatian politics', but it is noteworthy that there were differing interpretations of the concept of national unity. Some considered it to mean unity in action, whereas others considered it to mean unity in being – a unitarist notion of statehood, which would supersede the statehood rights of the component parts of the south slav state.[3] In the years preceding the First World War, the unitarists were dominant in Croatian politics.

Serbia, as an independent nation state, was the obvious focus for the realization of the south slav state, particularly after a number of advances towards the liberation of Serbs still under Ottoman rule in the early part of the twentieth century. Indeed, as Fred Singleton has pointed out, it was only in the early twentieth century that the idea of Serbia as 'the focal point for South Slav unification – a kind of Yugoslav Piedmont' gained significance within Serbia itself,[4] for in the nineteenth century the primary focus of the Serbs was the liberation of the Serbian people. While a number of Serbian leaders in the nineteenth century did promote the south slav idea, 'it was far from being a widely held concept until the twentieth century'.[5] By the twentieth century, of course, the struggle for Serbian independence – while narrower in conception than the south slav idea – had provided the base from which the idea could actually be realized, particularly after the strengthening of Serbia during the Balkan Wars.

The weakened and disintegrating Ottoman Empire found itself unable to maintain effective control of its territories in the Balkans. Having been administered by Austria since 1878, Bosnia was formally annexed in 1908 – a unilateral act which was received with great hostility by Serbia, given that Serbs constituted 40 per cent of the population of Bosnia. Within Bosnia itself there was considerable support for the idea of a south slav state under the leadership of Serbia, and many Bosnians fought with the Serbian and Montenegrin armies in the Balkan Wars of 1912–13. During these wars the Ottoman Empire was reduced to a tiny corner of the European landmass and Bulgaria was forced to cede most of Macedonia to Serbia, which also gained half of the Sanjak of Novibazar (a strip of land between Serbia and Montenegro). As a result of the Balkan Wars, Serbia almost doubled in size, and her population rose from 2.9 million to 4.4 million. Notwithstanding this increase in size and status, however, it was almost inconceivable that a south slav state could be created while the Austro-Hungarian Empire continued to exist: the context in which the south slav subjects of the Empire could be liberated just did not exist. However, the increasing strength and confidence of the Serbian state, together with its desire to liberate Bosnia from Austrian rule, set Serbia and Austria on a collision course. Austria was opposed to the emergence of a new power in the Balkans and was clearly determined to defeat the rising star of Serbia, as

Crnobrnja points out: 'Serbia was not only unsettling for its [Austria's] great-power interests but also promoted unrest among the Serbian and other Slavic subjects of the empire. The Habsburgs were opposed not only to Serbia but to the idea of Yugoslavism.'[6]

The opportunity came in 1914, when the Bosnian Serb Gavrilo Princip assassinated Franz Ferdinand, heir to the Austrian throne, when he was in Sarajevo to watch a military display. Princip's motivation was clear – as he stated at his trial: 'I am a Yugoslav nationalist, aiming for the unification of all Yugoslavs, and I do not care what form of state, but it must be free of Austria.'[7] Austria declared war on Serbia, but of course the matter did not end there. Four years later, the Austro-Hungarian Empire ceased to exist and thus the necessary conditions came into being for the creation of the south slav state.

THE WAR AND ITS OUTCOME

The war was a shattering experience for Serbia – a quarter of the population was lost – but it was also a war from which the Serbs emerged on the winning side and with an enormous stock of sympathy and admiration, for the odds against which they fought and against which they eventually emerged victorious. Serbia had faced a much larger and more powerful opponent; but the Serbs defeated the first two attacks and themselves launched counter-attacks into Bosnia. In many cases, the Serbs fought against fellow slavs conscripted into the imperial army. Although, by December 1914, Belgrade had been taken, this was a short-lived victory for the Empire, as their forces were subsequently defeated on the Kolubara River and Belgrade was recaptured.

As the war extended, however, Serbia could not sustain this position. With the entry of Bulgaria into the war, hoping to regain Macedonia, which it had lost to Serbia in the Balkan Wars, the odds increased against Serbia, and in October 1915, German, Austro-Hungarian and Bulgarian forces occupied the country after a six-week campaign. Occupied Serbia was divided between Austria-Hungary and Bulgaria. The experience of occupation was a terrible one. As Tim Judah writes:

> In addition to those sent to concentration camps in Hungary, some 30,000 Serbs were sent to Austrian camps or used as forced labour. Factories were plundered of their machinery and a dev-

astating typhus epidemic stalked the land ... Thousands died in desperate uprisings, and in some cases Bulgarian policy was so rigid that it even provoked mutinies among its own soldiers.[8]

Unwilling to passively accept occupation, a mass retreat was organized and undertaken by the government, army, king and thousands of civilians towards the Adriatic coast, where they were rescued by Allied forces. From the Albanian coast, the Serb army was evacuated by the French to Corfu, where thousands died in epidemics. From Corfu the survivors were taken to French Tunisia and subsequently to the Allied front in Salonika in Greece, where they fought alongside the Allies. At the end of the war they fought their way back to Belgrade with the French. Total Serbian losses in the war amounted to 275,000 military deaths and 800,000 civilian deaths as a result of war-time diseases and devastation. Two-thirds of the male population between the ages of 15 and 55 died.[9]

The massive upheaval of the war and the increasing likelihood of an Allied victory led to a resurgence of the aspiration for a south slav state to be formed out of the wreckage at the end of the war. To this end a Yugoslav Committee was constituted in London in April 1915 by a group of pro-Yugoslav leaders from Austria-Hungary. Their intention was to represent the south slavs of the Austro-Hungarian Empire and work for unity with Serbia. Indications that the Anglo-French Allies were planning to give away pieces of the south slav lands, to Italy and Bulgaria, in return for participation on the Allied side, led to outrage amongst the south slavs and acted as a catalyst for an agreement between them on the project of founding a Yugoslav state at the end of the war. In 1917, the Yugoslav Committee and the Serbian government, in exile in Corfu, signed the Corfu Declaration, calling for a kingdom of Serbs, Croats and Slovenes – a constitutional monarchy under the Serbian royal family. The document emphasized that 'anything less than the complete liberation of the South Slavs living under Habsburg rule, and their union with Serbia and Montenegro, was unacceptable'.[10]

On 1 December 1918 the Serbian Prince Regent Alexander proclaimed the new kingdom, on behalf of his father, King Peter. The proclamation was supported by the National Council in Zagreb (formed by the slavs of the Austro-Hungarian Empire) and by the Montenegrins who deposed their own king in order to join the new state. The moral high ground which the Serbs occupied thanks to their enormous war-time losses, combined with their obvious effectiveness at independent nation-building and the absence of any other real alternative in the post-war chaos, meant that the Serbs were pre-eminent in establishing the new state in a framework of their own choosing – basically more or less an expansion of the pre-war Serbian monarchy.

Yugoslavia could not have emerged without the backing of the victorious great powers – the United States, Britain and France. Their fundamental goal in endorsing the creation of Yugoslavia was the containment of Germany. The Allies backed the creation of a single Yugoslav state – under Serbian leadership – as a more effective bulwark against a revival of German ambitions in the Balkans than any collection of smaller states could possibly be. At the same time a larger unified south slav state would be more economically viable and therefore less susceptible to any extension of the Russian revolution into south-east Europe. Nonetheless, in the context of the severe economic problems of the inter-war period, Yugoslavia proved to be too weak to resist economic penetration by Germany in the 1930s.

The new state included the two independent kingdoms of Serbia and Montenegro, Croatia-Slavonia and the Vojvodina from the Hungarian part of the Austro-Hungarian Empire, Slovenia and Dalmatia from the Austrian part, Bosnia-Hercegovina from the joint Austro-Hungarian administration, and Macedonia and the Sanjak of Novibazar, which had been under Ottoman rule until the Balkan Wars of 1912 and 1913.

The state census of 1921 indicated that almost 84 per cent of the population was slav, albeit from differing backgrounds, and the remainder of the population was drawn from German, Hungarian, Albanian, Turkish, Romanian, Vlach, Roma and other communities. Religious affiliation cut across other lines of identity, so that the slav community was not homogeneous on a religious basis: Serbs, Montenegrins and Macedonians tended to be Orthodox Christians, Croats and Slovenes to be Catholics, and Bosnians to be Orthodox, Catholic or Muslim, following widespread conversion during the Ottoman period. In fact, the line dividing Orthodox and Catholic worlds cut through Yugoslavia, which comprised, in 1921, a population that was almost 47 per cent Orthodox and almost 40 per cent Catholic. A further complication was added by the fact that two different scripts were used within the new state: the Latin script was in use primarily in the former Austro-Hungarian territories, and the Cyrillic script in those lands previously under Ottoman domination. So, by any measure, the new Yugoslav state was a diverse and complex entity.

ECONOMIC CHALLENGES IN NATION-BUILDING

The new state had to integrate economies with different orientations and levels of development. The former Austro-Hungarian territories were the most economically advanced areas of the new kingdom, and suffered from the loss of the Austro-Hungarian Empire's market of around 60 million people within a much smaller and much less-developed Balkan economy. Serbia, on the other hand, which had experienced only limited industrial development in its central and northern areas, was now in a much larger market than previously. Montenegro and Macedonia were extremely underdeveloped and primarily engaged in subsistence farming. In policy terms, as Singleton and Carter have observed: 'The dominant Serbian group favoured a policy of economic autarchy, hoping to build manufacturing industries behind protective tariff walls and to use the resources of the state to promote industrial development.'[11]

In the early post-war years the government's efforts to encourage new industries met with some success. Industrial subsidies, protective tariffs and state credits, as well as mining concessions and the opening of state-owned mines fostered industrial development.[12]

Notwithstanding these early advances in industrialization, agriculture remained Yugoslavia's main source of trade revenue: with over 50 per cent of land officially defined as arable, she produced a diverse range of agricultural output, although her key crop was corn. As a result the Yugoslav economy remained particularly vulnerable to fluctuations in the international markets with agricultural, mineral and timber exports suffering enormously from the collapse of the international agricultural market in the mid-1920s. Initial attempts to overcome the collapse in prices through increased exports were dashed by the high tariffs of her previous customers.

The economic crash of 1929 was a catastrophe on a world-wide scale and one from which no country, including Yugoslavia, could hope to remain insulated. The contraction of foreign trade which followed the crash resulted in the value of the new state's exports and imports falling by over 60 per cent between 1929 and 1932.[13] The government response to this was to regulate the economy even more heavily, restricting imports and introducing fiscal measures. Even allowing for this external setback, however, the overall weakness of the economy was structural. The industrial sector remained small, concentrated around metallurgy and mineral production in Bosnia, Kosovo and Macedonia, and light-industrial sectors such as food-processing and textiles in Croatia and Slovenia.

From the mid-1930s there were the beginnings of economic recovery. Under Milan Stojadinovic the Yugoslav government tried to address the weaknesses of the industrial sector by increasing state regulation and investment in the transport infrastructure while, at the same time, seeking foreign investment to boost industrial and processed agricultural exports. He secured significant investment in mineral processing from Britain, France and Germany – through joint stock companies. However, as Singleton and Carter have noted, the drive towards industrialization based on foreign investment somewhat undermined Yugoslavia's economic independence.[14] In 1936 the German company Krupp successfully bid to run the Zenica iron works, developing it as a steel mill. Processing of raw materials within Yugoslavia nonetheless remained the exception with raw materials generally exported for processing. With regard to aluminium, for example:

> In 1937 Yugoslavia produced 350,000 tons of bauxite, of which it processed only 300 tons. Aluminium production was hampered by an agreement among world monopolies. Yugoslavia was singled out as the source of raw materials for certain German concerns, and was therefore prohibited from producing aluminium.[15]

By 1938 Yugoslavia's economy was two-thirds larger than before the First World War and industry accounted for 30 per cent of national income. The improvement in the economy was accompanied by Germany increasingly replacing France and others as a trading partner, and a loss of markets in France. Indeed, as Lampe observes: 'By 1935, Yugoslav exports to France had shrunk to less than 15 per cent of their 1930 level.'[16] In 1935 League of Nations sanctions against Italy over its invasion of Abyssinia allowed Germany to fill the gap created by loss of markets in Italy. At the same time, under Hitler, Germany was looking for sources of raw materials and embarking upon what Rothschild describes as its 'drive for economic hegemony over the Balkans'.[17] Yugoslavia's economy and industrialization process became increasingly tied to the demand for raw materials created by the German rearmament programme. 'It is undoubtedly true that the German rearmament programme stimulated trade and economic activity in Yugoslavia during the late 1930s.'[18]

By 1937 trade with Germany constituted a third of Yugoslavia's imports and exports. In 1938, Yugoslav bauxite provided 40 per cent of Germany's aluminium, and Germany was investing substantially in Yugoslav chrome and antimony extraction. German insistence on barter arrangements increased Yugoslav economic dependence. As Rothschild points out, Germany achieved 'a stranglehold on the Yugoslav economy, which virtually ceased to earn foreign credits in convertible foreign currencies'.[19]

In the agricultural sector Yugoslavia faced the typical problems of under-investment and overpopulation common to all the primarily agrarian states of the region. The traditional safety valve of rural emigration was closed by the restrictive immigration laws introduced by the United States in the early 1920s. It is calculated that, by 1931, up to 43 per cent of the rural population was surplus to the requirements of agricultural production.[20] At the same time the reduced flow of financial remittances from emigrants working overseas deepened rural poverty.

In common with the other new states in the region, which were all concerned to defuse peasant radicalism, Yugoslavia undertook a major land reform programme in 1919. Serfdom was abolished in Bosnia-Hercegovina and Macedonia. The large estates were broken up and redistributed to poor and landless peasants in Croatia-Slavonia and the Vojvodina. In Serbia and Montenegro the few large estates that had existed had already been abolished. However, the investment necessary to consolidate the land reform was not forthcoming. As Rothschild comments: 'In a country where over three-fourths of the population was engaged in agriculture and the bulk of state revenue was extracted from the peasants, the ministry of agriculture was habitually allocated only 1 per cent of the budget.'[21]

Peasant indebtedness was an enormous problem. The main lenders were private banks and moneylenders and it was not unusual 'that the peasant often bought in winter or spring at much higher prices from the storekeeper the very same grain that he had sold him after the preceding harvest, in payment of debt, and naturally, at a much lower price'.[22] By 1932, the worst year of the depression, this had reached crisis proportions with over 35 per cent of rural households in debt. The government was forced to declare a moratorium on peasant debt repayment and foreclosures. This provided short-term relief but it also meant that private banks and moneylenders were not prepared to advance further loans. As a result, without significant government assistance, investment in agriculture fell further. The countryside only began to recover in 1936 when the government decreed that the pre-1932 debts were halved and extended repayment over a 12-year period at a fixed, low rate of interest. This was accompanied by a programme of government support including rural public works, tax relief and cheap credit policies.

As in the industrial sector, economic revival was based upon a growing dependence on German markets. Germany became Yugoslavia's largest food exports customer: 'In 1938 Germany took 60 per cent of pig exports; more than 50 per cent of fresh meat; 99.5 per cent of wheat, and most of the hemp.'[23]

As Aldcroft and Morewood point out, the economic revival from the mid-1930s left Yugoslavia and other countries in eastern Europe 'highly vulnerable to political and economic pressure when market conditions deteriorated as they did later in the decade'.[24] Germany paid above world prices for the goods but payment was in Reichsmark balances, which could only be used to buy German products.[25]

POLITICAL CHALLENGES IN NATION-BUILDING

The inter-war period in Yugoslavia is often characterized as a conflict between Serbs and Croats over the nature of the state – whether it should be a unitary state under the leadership of Serbia, or whether it should be a federal state in which Croatia would have equality and autonomy. While the unitary/federal issue was undoubtedly an important one facing the country, it is an excessive polarization to suggest that positions on this were taken simply on the basis that Serbs sought a unitarist solution and Croats a federal one. Nevertheless, from the very beginning of the state there was strong and uncompromising hostility to a centralized, unitary state on the part of the largest Croat party, the Croatian Peasant Party, led by Stjepan Radic. However, Radic's abstentionist tactics often left other pro-federal forces weakened, thus weakening the forces opposed to centralizing tendencies.

The first governing body of Yugoslavia was the Interim National Legislature (INL), which had been provided for by the Corfu Declaration. This was largely appointed by regional assemblies or inter-party committees. Radic declined the two seats his Croatian Peasant Party had been allocated in the INL, and began what Crnobrnja describes as 'his open political confrontation' with Serbian centralism.[26] General elections to a Constituent Assembly took place in November 1920. The electoral campaign was primarily focused around the issue of centralism. The results, as Rothschild observes, showed that over half the elected deputies were from pro-unitarist parties (Radicals, Democrats and Agrarians) and less than a third were from pro-federalist and regional parties dominated by Croats, Muslims and Slovene Populists. The Communists formed the fourth largest group in the new Assembly.

Table 1.1   Elections to the Constituent Assembly, 28 November, 1920

Party	Number of votes	Percentage	Seats
Serbian Radical	284,575	17.7	89
Serbian Democrat	319,448	19.9	94
Serbian and Slovene Agrarian	151,603	9.4	39*
Croatian Peasant	230,590	14.3	50
Slovene Populist and Croatian Clerical	111,274	7.0	27
Bosniak Muslim (JMO)	110,895	6.9	24
Dzemijet Muslim	30,029	1.9	8
Communist	198,736	12.4	58
Social Democrat	46,792	2.9	10
Croatian bourgeois (four lists)	81,728	5.1	14
Other (nine lists)	41,865	2.5	6
Total	1,607,535	100.0	419

* Serbs received 30 seats and Slovenes, 9.
(taken from *East Central Europe between the Two World Wars*, by Joseph Rothschild, University of Washington Press, 1974)

The first sessions of the Assembly were characterized by conflict between a coalition of the two main centralist parties – the Radicals and Democrats – on the one hand, and federalist parties on the other. The Croatian Peasant Party was the third largest group in the Assembly but refused to participate, rejecting the oath of allegiance to the king, on the grounds that sovereignty should reside with parliament not the king. Through the boycott, as Rothschild points out, Radic's Croatian Peasant Party 'lost the chance to amend and affect the constitutional draft in committee or to persuade the Muslims and Slovene Agrarians to withhold their consent'.[27] The centralizers, under the leadership of Nikola Pasic, the dominant figure in the Serbian Radical-Democratic coalition – while gaining a victory for their preferred constitutional form – also contributed to deepening the conflict in the new state on this issue.

The constitution, adopted in June 1921, was legislatively unitarist but did allow for decentralized administration.[28] It was carried by 223 votes to 35, with 161 deputies either abstaining or boycotting the session. The majority comprised the Radical Party (old Serbia), the Democratic Party (Serbs from former Hapsburg lands), the Yugoslav Moslem Organization (from Bosnia-Hercegovina), the Dzemijet Party (of Macedonian and Albanian Muslims), and the Slovene Agrarian Party. The 35 votes against came primarily from the Serbian Agrarian Party and the Social Democrats. The other 161 deputies were made up of the Communist Party, Slovene Populists, Serbian Agrarians and others abstaining and the Croatian Peasant Party boycott.

PEASANTS AND COMMUNISTS

The Croatian Peasant Party had a very significant impact on Yugoslav politics in the 1920s. It was a typical example of the radical, populist, peasant-based parties which came to prominence in the region after the First World War. A comparable movement was the Bulgarian Agrarian National Union of Alexander Stamboliski, which was in government in Bulgaria in the early years after the First World War, enacting a radical, anti-bourgeois, anti-urban, political programme that was enormously popular amongst the overwhelmingly peasant population of the country, but which was eventually ousted in a coup by the former ruling elite in 1923. These radical agrarian parties tended to be anti-industrial, romanticizing the peasant and rural life as the true repository of the nation's soul. Without a coherent programme, Radic's Croatian

Peasant Party veered from affiliating to the Profintern, the Red Peasant International linked to the Comintern in 1924, to joining the government in 1925.

In fact, as Benson points out:

> The true beneficiaries of Radic's separatism were not the peasants, whose fortunes changed little, but the urban commercial classes in Croatia's cities, whose activities depended on resisting Belgrade's attempts to control foreign trade ... Whatever he may have said or intended, Radic was godparent to a purely bourgeois Croatian nationalism.[29]

The dominant Serbian parties favoured a regulated economy. They were not at all happy about the fact that Austrian and Hungarian assets comprised 60 per cent of Zagreb bank holdings.[30] Nevertheless, foreign investment in both Croatia and Slovenia increased during the 1920s, encouraging economic recovery and industrial development. By the mid-1920s, there was a shift in the nature of support for the Croatian Peasant Party. The extensive land reform, introduced by the Serbian Radical government, eased peasant dissatisfaction and their support for Radic's party dropped – and to some extent the party adapted to reflect the concerns of the new Croatian middle class, including participation in the political process to affect policy outcomes. The participation of the Croatian Peasant Party in government from 1925 ended Radic's radical phase.

The other radical party which emerged out of the social, political and economic meltdown of the First World War was the Communist Party of Yugoslavia (CPY). Formed in 1919, it won considerable support in the local and general elections in 1920, receiving 12.4 per cent of the vote in the elections to the Constituent Assembly in that year, with the fourth largest parliamentary bloc. Through its entire existence the CPY was committed to Yugoslavism on the basis of national equality within a unified state. As Rothschild points out, the CPY was

> the only major party whose appeal transcended ethnic and regional particularism. They alone affirmed the existence of a Yugoslav nation at a time when official nomenclature was still committed to the distinctiveness of its Serbian, Croatian and Slovene parts.[31]

Crnobrnja makes a similar point:

The CPY was ... truly Yugoslav, meaning that it had well-organised if small units all over the country. These were not the token representatives that some other parties also had in various parts of the country but lean and active organisations with a revolutionary purpose.[32]

The CPY was popular in both the most developed areas of the country, such as the Vojvodina and Dalmatia, and also in the most economically backward areas, notably Montenegro and Macedonia where it topped the poll. The government attempted to deal with the Communists by a policy of repression – designed to prevent the spread of revolution from Russia and later Hungary into the Balkans. When Communists won local elections in Belgrade and Zagreb the government used administrative methods to prevent them taking their seats. Political activity by the trade union and other organizations linked to the Communists were banned, following strikes and civil unrest. In 1921 the Communist Party was banned following an assassination attempt on the king for which the Communist Party denied any responsibility.

In Bulgaria, where Stamboliski's radical peasant regime introduced social and economic reforms, it is possible that an alliance between the Bulgarian Agrarian National Union and the popular Bulgarian Communist Party could have prevented Stamboliski's overthrow by the former ruling elite. Such an alliance did not take place – for which the BCP was subsequently taken to task for sectarianism by the Comintern, noting Lenin's emphasis on the worker–peasant alliance without which it would be impossible to command majority support in the predominantly agrarian societies of eastern Europe and the Balkans. The two main opposition parties in Yugoslavia, the Communist Party and the Croatian Peasant Party, making up a quarter of the parliament between them, were unable to contribute any meaningful alliance because of their dramatically different policies on the national question – with the Communists committed to Yugoslavism and Radic to Croatian nationalism. At the time of its ban, the CPY had 60,000 members and, though subsequently reduced in numbers, it continued to attract committed adherents in spite of harsh repression. Moreover, prolonged experience of underground work in these conditions made it better prepared than any other party in the country to survive and organize under the conditions of the Axis occupation during the Second World War.

ABSOLUTE RULE

On the parliamentary front, the 1920s were characterized by very frequent changes in government. In mid-1928 Radic was assassinated. At the beginning of 1929, King Alexander suspended the constitution, abolished parliament and declared absolute rule. He banned all political parties that had a 'tribal' or religious name or programme.[33] Alexander then pursued a policy of suppression of national and regional rights and enforced Yugoslavism, or 'integral' Yugoslavism, as he termed it. As Crnobrnja observes: 'This was the highpoint of the "oneness" of the newly emerging Yugoslav nation, but it was being accomplished in a way that could not hold.'[34] The name Yugoslavia was formally adopted and the state was divided into nine geographic units called *banovina*, which superseded the historic divisions in the country. Serbia was divided into five units and Croatia into two and all national flags and symbols were prohibited. The repression of national rights inevitably had the opposite results to those Alexander desired. One of the consequences of the dictatorship was the revival of separatist tendencies, both in Croatia and in Macedonia. In Crnobrnja's opinion,

> this was the moment they made their definitive break with the concept of Yugoslavia. Ante Pavelic, later to become the notorious leader of the Ustashi state, left Yugoslavia at this time, only to come back years later as head of the so-called Independent State of Croatia.[35]

The dictatorship also united representatives from all the communities of Yugoslavia in opposition to the king – including Serbs, Croats, Slovenes and Bosnian Muslims. This opposition, combined with external pressure from France,[36] led Alexander in 1931 to re-introduce a constitution. However, it consisted only of a National Assembly of parties acceptable, and subordinate, to the king. Alexander also created his own Yugoslav National Party funded and supported by the government. In 1932 there were widespread demands – from the Croatian opposition but also from throughout Yugoslavia, including Serbia – for a 'return to 1918 and the reconstitution of the state of Yugoslavia on a more equitable basis, eliminating Serbian hegemony'.[37] Alexander did not comply with these demands. In 1934 he was assassinated by an Ustasa-Macedonian terrorist group. This organization was sponsored by Mussolini's regime in Italy, which was keen on the break-up of Yugoslavia to further its own territorial expansion in the Balkans.

Elections in 1935 formally ended the dictatorship, but with the 1931 constitution still in place the party of government was ensured a majority and the three-man Regency, led by Alexander's brother, Prince Paul, had considerable power. The dominant Serbian political figure of the second half of the decade was Milan Stojadinovic, prime minister from 1935 to 1939, whose policy orientation was towards the Axis powers. His economic policies, as described above, in the context of international recovery from the trough of the depression, resulted in some economic improvements. At the same time, it also resulted in a growing dependence on Germany, with Yugoslavia becoming a cog in the German war machine. Stojadinovic was a defender of Alexander's repressive constitution of 1931, of the unitary state, and strongly anti-communist. As Benson points out, under his leadership, 'the government sent aid to Franco during the Spanish civil war'.[38] In 1937, after meeting Mussolini, he began to adopt fascist trappings but was never successful in establishing firm control either of his own party – the Yugoslav Radical Union – which he set up to supplant the Yugoslav National Party – or of parliament. Indeed, as Susan Woodward has pointed out: 'Yugoslavia was militantly anti-Bolshevik, but its fascist leanings, in contrast to those of its neighbours, were limited to the introduction of corporatist institutions in the economy and state.'[39] The old Serbian Radicals and the Yugoslav National Party were strongly against Stojadinovic's pro-Axis policies and at the beginning of 1939, Prince Paul put him out of office.

The removal of Stojadinovic was preceded by growing recognition that a more equitable arrangement between Croats and Serbs was essential if Yugoslavia was going to hold together. In 1937, the government had agreed in principle to a new constitution to this effect, but with the proviso that it would not come into effect until the king, Peter II, came of age. Under the new government in August 1939, an agreement or Sporazum was reached and the Banovina of Croatia was established, as Europe hovered on the brink of war. While the Croatian extreme right rejected the agreement and sought separation, it is notable that this was still a very marginal position. On the eve of the German invasion of Yugoslavia, Vladimir Macek, leader of the Croatian Peasant Party – as Crnobrnja describes him, 'the undisputed leader of mainstream Croatian politics'[40] – was offered independent statehood for Croatia, outside Yugoslavia, by the Germans. Macek, who was one of the authors of the Sporazum, declined the offer and did not wish to seek a solution outside Yugoslavia.

The Sporazum was accompanied by requests for greater regional autonomy from other areas. Such developments were cut off by the onset of the Second World War, however, and Yugoslavia, along with the wider region, was immediately Balkanized by the German occupiers. Yugoslavia was fragmented into a number of smaller units, which were intended to pose no threat to German economic and strategic interests. Under the leadership of Tito, however, the Communist partisan resistance movement simultaneously fought to liberate the south slav peoples, reunify the country and introduce a political, social and economic system which would ensure self-determination and independence, and resolve the national question. These goals were achieved and the reunification of the south slav state was achieved in 1945 with the creation of the federal republic under the leadership of the Communist Party of Yugoslavia.

2
The Second World War

The victorious powers of the First World War had supported the foundation of the Yugoslav state, in part to act as a Balkan bulwark against a potentially resurgent Germany. For Yugoslavia to succeed in this role, it would need considerable diplomatic and economic support to enable rapid industrialization and development. Economic backing was forthcoming to some extent during the 1920s, but was cut off following the 1929 crash. During the depression the economic relationship between Yugoslavia and Serbia's traditional allies, Britain and France weakened. Both withdrew financial credits. Under Hitler after 1933, Germany moved to try to step into the vacuum in order to gain access to raw materials from the Balkans. The balance of power in Europe had started to shift after 1933 with the victory of Nazism in Germany. The standing of Britain and France was weakened, which damaged their strategy of containing Germany and opposing Soviet communism by promoting the anti-revisionist alliance systems of the Little Entente and Balkan Entente, both of which relied on French support and in which Yugoslavia participated.

Mussolini's regime – which had extensive ambitions in the Balkans – was no longer politically isolated, which was a very dangerous factor for Yugoslavia. The increasing influence of Germany in central Europe meant that revision of the Versailles territorial settlement in eastern Europe was virtually certain. There were many claims on Yugoslav territory, but the greatest danger came from Italy, which had designs on the Adriatic coast, and in the inter-war period had supported the Ustasa, the Croatian fascist movement, because it sought an independent Croatia, which would lead to the break-up of Yugoslavia and the fulfilment of Italy's territorial ambitions. Indeed, the danger of domination or absorption by Italy had been one of the key factors in Slovenia opting to join the south slav state at the end of the First World War.

During the 1930s Germany's main concern was with the efficient supply of industrial raw materials and agricultural produce and the status quo in Yugoslavia was tolerated as long as these supplies were uninterrupted. The coup of April 1941 against the Regent Paul's secret pact with Hitler, however, threatened German dominance. Germany responded by bombing and invading Yugoslavia. The state was broken up and occupied by Germany, Italy, Hungary and Bulgaria – all committed to tearing up the Versailles settlement – including the establishment of an independent Croatian state incorporating Bosnia-Hercegovina under the fascist Ustasa but in reality controlled by Italy and Germany.

The war was a time of extraordinary suffering in which 11 per cent of the population, or 1,700,000 Yugoslavs, perished.[1] This enormous toll was equivalent as a proportion of the population only to the Soviet Union's losses. This was a high price, but it was also a significant contribution to the eventual allied victory, for the resistance movement held down 30 divisions of enemy troops during a crucial period of the war.[2] It was in the context of the resistance which developed to the Axis occupation and genocidal policies that the Communist Party of Yugoslavia, under the leadership of Josip Broz Tito, was able to gain support and emerge at the end of the war as the leader of the resistance movement and the dominant political force in the country. As Susan Woodward observes: 'Nationalist anti-imperialism of the nineteenth century had ... been revived as a shared bond among Yugoslav peoples, although it had now taken the form of anti-fascism under Communist party leadership.'[3]

THE EVE OF WAR

The orientation of Hitler and Germany's Axis allies was clear – to achieve colonial domination of east and south-east Europe and the Soviet Union. As Yugoslav leaders met to agree the forming of the Croatian Banovina, Europe was moving rapidly towards war. The Nazis entered Prague in March 1939, dividing Czechoslovakia and creating a Slovakian puppet state, and in April Italy annexed Albania. In September the Nazis invaded Poland and Yugoslavia declared its neutrality, which was a difficult position to sustain, particularly after the surrender of France in June 1940. Concessions were made to Nazi Germany in October in an attempt to maintain the status quo, not only economically, but also through anti-semitic laws restricting Jewish participation in education and banning them from participation in food industries, although these did not apply to the children of Jews 'who had fought in defence of the state'.[4] However, in strong contrast with most of her neighbours, there was negligible support for overt fascist or anti-semitic parties within Yugoslavia. In the elections of 1938 the Serbian fascist list polled only 1 per cent of the vote, winning no seats. As Leslie Benson has observed: 'no major political grouping singled out Jews for perse- cution as a matter of overt policy, so that they enjoyed a flourishing cultural and religious life, largely unmolested'.[5]

Towards the end of October 1940 Mussolini invaded Greece in a disastrous campaign whose conclusion required the intervention of the German army. From that point the rest of south-eastern Europe was rapidly caught up in the war: Romania and Hungary signed the Tripartite Pact of Japan, Germany and Italy in November 1940, and Bulgaria signed at the beginning of March 1941. The Yugoslav Regent, Paul, was put under intense pressure by the Nazis to join the Pact and was promised that Yugoslavia would be guaranteed her territorial integrity, freedom from occupation and non-combatant status. The country was now surrounded by Axis supporters or occupied nations. German occupation of the Czech lands blocked Yugoslav access to the Skoda works, her main arms supplier. As Rothschild points out: 'The British were prodigal with exhortations to the Yugoslavs to preserve their honour by rebuffing the Germans, but short on the military assistance that might have given weight to this advice.'[6] Paul is reported to have told the US Ambassador: 'You big nations are hard. You talk of our honour, but you are far away.'[7]

Paul signed up to the Pact on 25 March 1941, and when this became known, the regime was overthrown by a military coup on 27 March under the leadership of the air force. Paul was deposed and sent into exile, to be replaced by the young king, Peter, who was declared to have come of age, and prime minister Cvetkovic was replaced by air-force general Dusan Simovic. The coup was extremely popular in Belgrade as it rejected Paul's capitulationist stance to what was still seen by most Serbs as their First World War enemy. According to Singleton: 'there is evidence of widespread opposition to Paul's foreign policy, from all parts of the country and from all political groups'.[8] Simovic and his cabinet did attempt to avert German retribution – they did not renounce the Pact, but simultaneously began talks with both the British and the Soviets. The former discussion did not produce the practical aid the

Yugoslavs hoped for. Hitler had ordered on the day of the coup that: 'Yugoslavia should be attacked, defeated with all speed, and Belgrade subjected to exemplary punishment by air bombardment.'[9]

The German attack began on 6 April 1941. The Luftwaffe bombed Belgrade, killing around 10,000 people and destroying large parts of the city, and the German army entered Yugoslavia with Hungarian and Bulgarian forces. On 10 April the Ustasa declared the Independent State of Croatia. On 12 April Belgrade fell to the invading armies, and on 17 April the Yugoslav Army surrendered after ten days of blitzkrieg. The government fled into exile, via Athens and Jerusalem, to London. The Yugoslav Army lost more than 3,000 men in those ten days and the German less than 200. Yet, although the German losses were small, the attack was nevertheless significant, for the invasion of Yugoslavia probably delayed the invasion of the Soviet Union by at least a month when time was at a premium.

DIVISION AND OCCUPATION

Yugoslavia as a state ceased to exist. It was divided between various Axis powers with two puppet states of Croatia and Serbia occupied by Italy and Germany. The so-called Independent State of Croatia under a puppet Italian king – Tomislav II, the nephew of Victor Emmanuel III – incorporated Bosnia-Hercegovina, and was divided on an east–west basis with German military control to the north and Italian to the south. The rump state of Serbia, was under German military occupation and the puppet leadership of General Milan Nedic. The other parts of Yugoslavia were parcelled out amongst the occupying powers: Slovenia was divided between Germany and Italy; the Dalmatian coast from Zadar to Split to Italy; Montenegro to Italy; parts of Vojvodina, and lands north of the Drava and Danube to Hungary; Kosovo and western Macedonia to Italian-run Albania; the Banat under German administration; and eastern Macedonia to Bulgaria. In other words, the territorial aspirations and revisions of the defeated powers since Versailles, were now broadly fulfilled – although there were some grumbles about the share-out, and Yugoslavia ceased to exist. As Phyllis Auty has pointed out: 'The divided territory was meant to give Germany strategic control over the whole region and political control through a policy of divide and rule.'[10] In other words Yugoslavia was well and truly Balkanized. However, although the German aim was certainly achieved in the short term, eventually the fragmentation of administration and control led to a weakening of the occupying forces, which the resistance movement was able to exploit.

Within Serbia, the Nazis took immediate steps to establish full control. Nearly 200,000 army officers and men were deported to prisoner-of-war camps in Germany, and a new police force was set up, recruited from the ethnic German population in the Vojvodina. Strict curfews and other restrictions were imposed including the registration of all Jews with the police, and concentration camps were set up around Belgrade.[11] In Kosovo, Kosovan Albanians wreaked death and destruction on Serbs and Montenegrins in the region and tens of thousands fled to Serbia.[12]

Ante Pavelic, leader of the Croatian fascist Ustasa party, returned to Zagreb from Italy, and assumed leadership of the new enlarged Independent State of Croatia – which, out of a population of 6.3 million, included 1.9 million Serbs and 0.75 million Muslims. The creation of this state, which was welcomed by leading cleric Cardinal Stepinac, was declared by the Nuremberg Tribunal to be a major war crime.[13] As Lampe observes, however, total support for the Ustasa, 'was still less than 10 per cent of politically active Croats, significantly less than their counterparts, the Hungarian Arrow Cross and the Romanian Iron Guard'.[14] However, because of their support in government by the occupying German and Italian forces, they were able to visit barbarism upon Serbs, Jews and Roma, out of all proportion to their number and support in Croatia. The Ustasa goal was a racially pure state from which Serbs, Jews and Roma would be eradicated, and they went to great lengths to actually achieve this. Massacres of Serbs in the Krajina – including women and children – began in April 1941 and mass deportations in early June. As Judah observes, 'in Croatia and Bosnia fanatical Serb-hating Ustashas were on the loose, perpetrating appalling massacres which quickly led to Serbian uprisings and the loss of control over large areas'.[15] Jews were made to wear identification, banned from public facilities and pressed into forced labour. Estimates vary as to the scale of the killing, but by the end of the war it is likely that half a million or more Serbs, Jews and Roma had been murdered in local massacres, killed in small camps and at the two major concentration camps at Jasenovac and Stara Gradiska or sent to their deaths at Auschwitz.

Opposition to this appalling regime was articulated by pre-war Croatian leaders, as well as some of the Bosnian Muslim leadership. Macek, the leader of the Croatian Peasant Party, refused to lend public support to the regime, and was sent to Jasenovac. The atrocities perpetrated by the Ustasa were so terrible that the Italian occupying forces on occasion intervened to protect the Serbs and even reoccupied areas that had been previously put under the direct control of the Ustasa regime. There were even cases, as Judah points out, of 'the Italians having certain senior Ustashas arrested and shot'.[16] Not surprisingly, when the Partisan resistance movement entered the Independent State of Croatia in summer 1942, they were welcomed and joined by many Croats and Bosnians, helping to give the movement what was ultimately to be its all-Yugoslav composition.

RESISTANCE

In the early months of the occupation, organized resistance began to take shape. General Staff officer Colonel Draza Mihailovic began to bring together a loosely organized Chetnik movement – the name originally given to guerrilla bands and then used as the name for King Alexander's local militias under the dictatorship. He gathered about 10,000 men in western Serbia and asked the Yugoslav government-in-exile for recognition as an army that would both fight the occupiers and defend Serbs from Ustasa atrocities in Bosnia and Croatia.[17] Mihailovic received official status – in 1942 the government-in-exile named him minister of war and army chief of staff – and he was, initially, supported by the British. Eventually, however, it became apparent that he was not actively pursuing resistance – indeed there is evidence that he collaborated with the Germans and Italians, considering the larger Communist-led resistance, rather than the occupiers, as his main enemy.

The largest and only really effective Yugoslav resistance was the Communist Party-led Partisans, under the leadership of Tito, who was eventually to go on to lead Yugoslavia until his death in 1980. Born Josip Broz, of a Croatian father and a Slovene mother, in Kumrovec in the Croatian lands of the Austro-Hungarian Empire in 1892, Tito was the seventh child of a peasant family, which owned about ten acres of land. His reasons for becoming a communist 'lay in the injustices of society, the poverty and oppression he had seen as a child'.[18] In the early 1920s he worked as a political organizer for the Yugoslav Communist Party and was then arrested in 1928, and imprisoned. A year after his release, in 1935, he went to Moscow to work for the Comintern, subsequently returning to Yugoslavia and becoming General Secretary of the Communist Party in 1939. He was an extremely able military and political leader who was much admired beyond the communist political framework. The Partisans began their operations on 4 July, shortly after the Nazi invasion of the Soviet Union on 22 June 1941, although preparations were already underway prior to this. Tito arrived in Belgrade on 8 May 1941 to organize the forces. Between April and July, the Communist Party grew from 8,000 to 12,000 members, and the Communist Youth organization reached 30,000 members.[19] On 27 June the Communist Party leadership set up the General Headquarters of National Liberation Partisans' Detachments and on 4 July converted the party leadership into a military General Staff, indicating their intention to create an army. The goal of the Partisan movement was the defeat of the Axis occupation, but the Communist Party was well aware that the post-war political settlement and social order would also be at stake. The Soviet leadership and the Comintern clearly advised against immediate revolutionary goals. As the Bulgarian Comintern leader Georgi Dimitrov put it: 'Remember that at present it is a question of liberation from Fascist domination and not a question of Socialist revolution.'[20]

Nevertheless, as the resistance movement against the Axis occupiers progressed, it became entwined with a social revolution and civil war against the supporters of the pre-war monarchy who regarded preservation of the economic, social and political pre-war order as paramount. Tito recognized that only through south slav unity could real independence be achieved and that this in turn would be impossible without scrupulous respect and equality between the different nationalities. This was a radically different approach to the pre-war suppression of national political expression. Huge emphasis was placed on the primacy of equality and brotherhood, as Judah observes:

> In Bosnia, the Partisan rallying cry was for a country that was to be 'neither Croatian nor Serbian, nor Moslem, but Serbian and Moslem and Croatian'. It was to be 'a free and brotherly Bosnia

and Hercegovina, in which full equality of all Serbs, Moslems and Croats will be ensured'.[21]

Tito's communist Partisan movement set about achieving these aims, always, as John R. Lampe points out, 'considering themselves a Yugoslav rather than a Serbian movement'.[22] In May 1941 leaders of the Slovenian and Croatian Communist Parties – which were organized on a confederal basis within the Yugoslav Party – met with Tito in Belgrade to discuss a Yugoslav-wide approach to resistance. Tito's vision was of a

National Liberation Anti-Fascist Front of all the peoples of Yugoslavia, regardless of party or religion. In forming partisan detachments it is essential not to be narrow-minded, but to give wide scope to initiative and enterprise of every kind.[23]

There were some early initiatives by Mihailovic and Tito to explore the possibility of working together. They met in September 1941 and agreed to cooperate at a local level. Some joint operations took place, but this rapidly broke down. In Singleton's view this was 'partly because of disagreement over ultimate political objectives'.[24] There was also disagreement over resistance strategy. The Chetniks treated the Partisans as enemies as much, or more, as they treated the Germans and attempted to preserve their forces for the denouement they expected at the end of the war in the fight over the social and political order which would follow. The German High Command prescribed ferocious German reprisals against the Yugoslav civilian population when German forces were attacked. One hundred Yugoslav civilians were to be killed for every one German soldier killed, and 50 killed for every German wounded. This policy was carried out with the utmost severity, as in Kragujevac in October 1941, where 7,000 civilians were killed, including several hundred schoolboys.[25] This reinforced the passive policy of Mihailovic's Chetniks. The Partisans on the other hand grasped that, while adventurism must be rejected, the resistance could not simply wait for others to liberate their country. As Vladimir Dedijer, a leading Partisan wrote of his experience with the Chetniks:

I had great difficulty persuading the Chetnik commanders around Kragujevac to take part in the fighting against the Germans. They said they had no orders. On the other hand they criticized our command because we 'wasted mercilessly the blood of the Serbian people fighting against the Germans in an uneven struggle'. They advised us that we should wait until the Germans were weaker before fighting against them.[26]

Dedijer acknowledged, however, that some Chetnik units did fight the Germans, and in some cases joined the Partisans in order to continue doing so. However, this was not the main tendency within the Chetnik movement. Benson makes the following observations:

it was clear from the outset that the Partizans were their main enemy – it was the Chetniks, not the Germans, who first attacked the Partizans around Uzice, at the beginning of November 1941. Mihailovic was therefore willing to enter into negotiations with the Nedic regime, and some of his fighters became 'legals', that is, a Serbian quisling force under Nedic, in order to fight the Communists.[27]

The Partisans pressed ahead with their campaign, establishing 'people's governments' in the areas that they liberated from occupation, where thousands of people's committees operated as local government and women were granted the right to vote for the first time.[28] The people's committees took responsibility for many aspects of the running of daily life, including education, taxation, food distribution, wages and prices, repairs and rebuilding, and they formed the basis for post-war local government. The conduct of the Partisan forces was rigorously enforced, which contributed significantly to the level of support they won from the local population. As Auty comments:

Their Spartan behaviour was commented on with wondering admiration by all Allied officers assigned to Partisan units in the latter part of the war ... Looting and theft – even in the smallest degree – were punished, after summary trial, by execution.[29]

The Partisans were forced out of their main base in Uzice – known as the Uzice Republic – in November 1941, and moved headquarters into Bosnia where the restructuring of the military organization began, by mid-1942 forming the Proletarian Brigades, which became the core of the Yugoslav People's Army. In November 1942 the Anti-Fascist Council of National Liberation of Yugoslavia (AVNOJ) was convened in Bihac in western Bosnia, attended by representatives of the national liberation movement from all over Yugoslavia. Its aim was 'the liberation of Yugoslavia and the establishment of a broad democratic government, which recognised the rights of the different ethnic and religious groups in the country'.[30] AVNOJ was effectively to form the basis of the post-war government.

In response to these developments, the occupying forces began a determined offensive against the Partisan forces in January 1943, driving them out of Bosnia and into Montenegro. The Partisans were joined during this period by the British military mission, Captains William Deakin and William Stuart. Deakin and Stuart were parachuted to the Partisan HQ on Mount Durmitor at a time of intense fighting during which Stuart was killed and both Deakin and Tito were wounded. While politically and ideologically more sympathetic to the Chetniks, the British government was coming to accept that the only militarily effective resistance was the Partisans. Partisan fortunes rose rapidly as the Italian regime collapsed in September of 1943 and her forces were instructed to surrender to the Partisans. This meant both a massive influx of arms and supplies, and also some soldiers as Italians joined the Partisans, forming Garibaldi Divisions in the Partisan army.[31] There was also increased support from the Allied forces in Italy. By November 1943 the Partisans had recaptured considerable amounts of territory in Dalmatia and Bosnia, and on 29 November held the second meeting of AVNOJ at Jajce in Bosnia. Dedijer describes this meeting as the most important event of the war, 'for it was there that the foundations of the new state were laid'.[32] At this meeting a National Committee was established as the executive body of AVNOJ, with the powers of a provisional government. The government-in-exile in London ceased to have any power within Yugoslavia, and it was decided that the question of the future of the monarchy would be decided after the war. Perhaps most important, 'the principle was proclaimed that Yugoslavia was to be a federated state'.[33] The National Committee and Presidium of AVNOJ were constituted on a broad political basis from the national liberation movement. The President of AVNOJ was Ivan Ribar, a member of the Democratic Party who had been Speaker of the Yugoslav Constituent Assembly in 1921, who had joined the Partisan movement on its foundation. Tito was President of the National Committee and responsible for national defence. Dusan Sernec, a leader of the Catholic Clerical Party of Slovenia, became

Commissioner for Finance, and Vlado Zecevic, a former Chetnik commander, was made Commissioner for Internal Affairs.[34] The Soviet leadership was annoyed by this decision by AVNOJ to declare itself the political leadership of the state, rejecting all claims of the government-in-exile in London. Soviet concerns hinged around their desire to maintain good relations with the other Allies, prior to the conclusion of the war and the post-war settlement. Tito received many reproaches from Moscow for his pursuit of the social and political revolution in Yugoslavia, but he was not significantly deterred from his course.

It was at this time that the Allies made the final decision to channel all support to the Partisans and cease supplying Mihailovic – the British now had evidence that his forces had not been effectively fighting the enemy, but had instead been collaborating with them in order to defeat the Partisans. The British military mission led by Fitzroy Maclean arrived in Bosnia soon after the Italian surrender and he conveyed very positive reports of Partisan activity back to Churchill. The Allied leaders met at Teheran at the same time as the AVNOJ meeting, and it was there that they agreed that Tito was the key player, both in war-time victory, and effectively, in the future Yugoslavia. The government-in-exile attempted to adapt to this new situation, withdrawing support from Mihailovic and urging support for Tito. In June 1944 a new royal government was formed under the leadership of Ivan Subasic, with the aim of reaching agreement with Tito. That same month Subasic went to visit Tito and met the whole National Committee, where he suggested that the National Committee should be incorporated into the Royal Yugoslav Government and asserted that King Peter was the commander of all armed forces in Yugoslavia. Not surprisingly, the Partisans rejected Subasic's suggestion, and Josip Smodlaka, Commissioner of Foreign Affairs, pointed out to him that: 'You have neither people, nor army, nor territory.'[35] Eventually, Subasic agreed to recognize the National Committee and the National Liberation Army as the only authority and the only army in Yugoslavia and members of Subasic's government were incorporated into the AVNOJ provisional government.

Mihailovic was unwilling to accept the new settlement and in January 1944 held a congress of anti-communist forces in the village of Ba in Serbia, proposing the establishment, post-war, of a federal Yugoslavia under Serb domination. However, Mihailovic's collaboration with the enemy – largely because of his rabid anti-communism – meant that he had completely lost any patriotic credibility he might have had at the beginning of the war, when he attempted to rally local forces against the occupiers.

His attempts to pose an alternative to AVNOJ came to nothing – a reality he was reluctant to accept. In fact, his active opposition was only ended in March 1946, when he was captured after attempting to continue military resistance to the new government. He was tried for collaborating with the German and Italian occupiers and with the Serbian puppet regime under General Nedic and executed.

In September 1944, Tito met with Stalin and Molotov in Moscow, to discuss arrangements for the final liberation of Yugoslavia. It was agreed that the Red Army would only enter Yugoslavia

> for the limited campaigns necessary for its advance through central Europe, and that Yugoslav forces should undertake operations simultaneously and join the Red Army in the advance on Belgrade. It was also agreed that the Soviet forces should have no administrative or civil powers in Yugoslavia.[36]

This last factor turned out to be crucial for the ability of the Yugoslav Communist Party to secure the type of post-war social and political order for which they had fought. In October 1944 Belgrade was liberated by the Partisans – Tito entered the city at the head of an army of 300,000 men and women – together with the Soviet Red Army, on its way west from Bulgaria and Romania.[37]

THE COST OF THE WAR

The human costs of the war were enormous, with 1,700,000 or 11 per cent of the pre-war population dead – the average age of the dead was 22 years. The economy was completely dislocated. As Singleton and Carter have observed: 'There was no longer a Yugoslav economy', and normal economic life had ceased to exist, giving way to a barter economy.[38] According to UNRAA figures, 3,500,000 people were homeless.[39] Agricultural production dropped in all areas. In the least affected areas, such as Bulgarian-occupied Macedonia, or German-occupied Slovenia, or Hungarian-occupied Vojvodina, the percentage decrease in output of cereals and cattle, comparing 1943 with 1935–7, was around 20 per cent. The worst affected area was Bosnia-Hercegovina, annexed by the Independent State of Croatia, where the output decrease was 60 per cent in cereals and 50 per cent in cattle. In German-occupied Serbia, the percentage decrease in both cereals and cattle was 40 per cent.[40] Some industrial production was maintained by the occupying forces for their own requirements, but the destruction of the country's infrastructure was enormous. According to UNRAA figures, 822,000 buildings were destroyed, of which 289,000 were peasant dwellings, and 80 per cent of ploughs and agricultural equipment were destroyed. The transport infrastructure was also very hard hit – with 50 per cent of railway lines, 77 per cent of locomotives and 84 per cent of goods wagons destroyed. This was the context in which Tito and the AVNOJ provisional government had to unite and rebuild the country.

3
The Tito years

The united federal state under the leadership of Tito was widely accepted within Yugoslavia, and the country was rapidly stabilized and set upon a process of social and economic recovery. The most important challenge to the country in the aftermath of the war came from an unexpected quarter, the Soviet leadership, which took exception to Tito's political independence and refusal simply to follow the policies laid down by Moscow. Tito's assertion of political independence in the face of Stalin's attempts to ensure Yugoslav compliance resulted in the withdrawal of Soviet assistance and veiled threats of intervention. In order to survive in these circumstances, Tito attempted a balance between the west and Moscow. In the context of the Cold War geopolitical framework, even a communist Yugoslavia as a chink in the Soviet bloc which the US sought to widen using economic aid to Yugoslavia was a lever. Susan Woodward argues that:

> The regime survived thanks to U.S. military aid; U.S.-orchestrated economic assistance from the International Monetary Fund, World Bank, U.S. Export-Import Bank, and foreign banks; and the restoration of trade relations with the west after August 1949. In exchange, socialist Yugoslavia played a critical role for U.S. global leadership during the cold war: as a propaganda tool in its anti-communist and anti-Soviet campaign and as an integral element of NATO's policy in the eastern Mediterranean.[1]

This, however, exaggerates the position. Tito never joined the NATO camp, he simply exploited the Cold War antagonism to sustain political independence from Moscow and the west whilst constructing a socialist-oriented society at home.

Relations with the Soviet Union improved after Stalin's death and this allowed renewed trade links with the CMEA countries to develop. However, first under Ronald Reagan and then at the end of the 1980s with the collapse of communism in eastern Europe, Washington radically shifted its tactical orientation to Yugoslavia

– first tightening the financial screw and later intervening diplo-
matically and finally militarily to destroy the Yugoslav federation.

Meanwhile, from the 1950s Tito initiated radical reforms to the
Yugoslav socialist system – self-management, in both economic
and political spheres. Throughout his years in power Tito also
attempted with some success to create a genuine and functioning
equality between the constituent nations of the federal republic.
This was enshrined in the country's post-war constitutions.
However, economic and political decentralization reforms in the
late 1960s and 1970s strengthened the centrifugal tendencies
within the republics to the detriment of federal government and
weakened the ability of the state to ensure investment in industry
and control of inflation. Once subjected to the external pressures
exerted through the IMF, these factors contributed significantly to
the economic problems, which came to a head in the 1980s.
Economic crisis engendered tensions over the division of national
income between republics and with the federal government, which
in turn encouraged the development of nationalist tendencies at
republican level. In this context the financial pressures exerted by
the IMF were supplemented by covert German and Austrian
assistance to nationalist groups, including in some cases the
supplying of aid to armed separatists. This had a destabilizing
impact, which, combined with the economic problems that the
country faced, eventually presented a serious threat to the
continued unity of Yugoslavia.

ESTABLISHING THE NEW STATE

In its first post-war reincarnation, Yugoslavia was known as
Democratic Federative Yugoslavia. The AVNOJ provisional
government ran the country – until the first elections for the Constituent Assembly in November 1945 – and introduced some key
laws, firmly establishing the political framework for the new state
on the military and political achievements of the Partisan
movement. Mihailovic's supporters were rapidly defeated and the
property of collaborators was expropriated. All citizens over the
age of 18 received the right to vote. An agrarian reform was
introduced, establishing the size of landholdings as between 20
and 35 hectares.

Very little of the pre-war administrative systems survived the war, and the Communist Party, together with the local People's Committees which had been organized by the Partisans in liberated areas, carried out the functions of local government. In August 1945 the People's Front was formed, which was effectively a continuation of the AVNOJ in an electoral form, including many of the non-communists who had participated in the resistance movement throughout Yugoslavia. Attempts made by some politicians from parties outside the Front – such as the Democratic Party and the Croatian Peasant Party – to organize an opposition failed, and in the end they did not participate in the election. The only list of candidates put to the voters was the People's Front list and it was overwhelmingly endorsed. As Fred Singleton has observed: 'Less than 10 per cent of those who went to the polls rejected the official list. In the absence of opposition candidates the election was in reality a plebiscite.'[2]

The new Assembly established Yugoslavia as the Federative People's Republic of Yugoslavia and dispensed with the monarchy. The country's first new constitution was accepted in January 1946. This established six federal republics: Serbia, Croatia, Slovenia, Bosnia-Hercegovina, Macedonia and Montenegro. Two autonomous regions were established within Serbia – the province of Vojvodina and the district of Kosovo-Metohija. Each republic had the formal right to secede.

The Federal Assembly had two components: the Federal Council, which was elected by the entire voting population, and the Council of Nationalities, which was elected by the parliaments of the six republics and the two autonomous regions within Serbia. The Assembly's Presidential Council functioned as a collective head of state. The constitution also gave legal status to the People's Committees and their direct and participatory democracy was considered to have been one of the great achievements of the national liberation struggle. The People's Committees were subsequently to play an increasing role during the development and establishment of self-management. The constitution also set out the basic principles for the state-directed economy that was being constructed within Yugoslavia, establishing state control of mineral resources, power, communication and foreign trade, within the framework of a 'general economic plan' for the development of the country.[3]

The immediate post-war period was one of highly centralized government, as urgent attempts were made to feed and house the people and reconstruct the economy and society. UNRAA aid was essential, 'which provided food for between three and five million people during the winter of 1945–6, as well as clothing, medical supplies, seed, livestock, jeeps, railway wagons and locomotives, to the value of $60 million'.[4] In the subsequent two to three years, state ownership and control were established over large enterprises, industry, transport and financial institutions, while most agricultural land remained privately owned, as did many small businesses.

THE SPLIT WITH THE SOVIET UNION

To the outside observer, Yugoslavia appeared to be following the Soviet political and economic model – a pattern which was emerging across the countries of central and eastern Europe. However, a rift emerged publicly between Yugoslavia and the Soviet Union in 1948, with Yugoslavia being expelled from the Cominform – the organization of ruling communist parties set up in 1947. The charges levelled against the Yugoslav Communist Party were primarily to do with the nature and pace of the political and economic reforms taking place within Yugoslavia. They were simultaneously accused of being leftist with regard to the rapid nationalization of retail outlets, and of '"taking the path of a populist, kulak party" in its dealings with the peasantry'.[5] As Singleton and Carter point out, however, this was rather an odd criticism coming from the Cominform, as none of the other newly communist countries of eastern Europe had collectivized by 1948, and most allowed private farmers to own more land than the maximum in Yugoslavia under the 1945 land reform. The Yugoslav Communist Party was also criticized at great length for diluting itself as a vanguard party and subordinating itself to the People's Front. In the year prior to the public expulsion from the Cominform, the Yugoslav Communist Party was subjected to ferocious political attack in the pages of the Cominform newspaper, *For a lasting peace, For a people's democracy*, to which the Yugoslav leadership attempted to respond in theoretical terms. Their determination to argue their position led eventually to their being labelled as Trotskyists, fascist agents and so on. Other communist parties were also required to criticize Tito – in Britain, in 1951, the

Communist Party published *From Trotsky to Tito*, a regurgitation of Soviet views written by James Klugmann, one of the Communist Party's leading theoreticians. The book was withdrawn in 1956 when Khrushchev apologized to Tito.

The real issue that led to the split was not, however, differences over the pace of reform, but differences over Tito's assertion of political independence, including foreign policy. The Soviet Union emerged from the Second World War as a victor power – indeed, given its role in destroying the great bulk of Hitler's armies, as the dominant European military force on the continent. The Soviet leadership also enjoyed broad political prestige in both eastern and western Europe as a result of its decisive role in defeating Germany and the leading position of communists in resistance movements amid the deep discredit attached to the broad collaboration of western and eastern European pre-war party circles with the Axis occupying regimes. Stalin was concerned to consolidate a Soviet sphere in eastern Europe as a buffer against any resurgence of Germany. Given the military and political balance of forces which emerged from the war, the west was in no position to prevent this. This was the reality behind the famous percentage agreement between Churchill and Stalin in Moscow in October 1944, where they agreed on the division of influence in the countries of eastern Europe. What this showed Stalin, however, was that Churchill accepted the reality of Soviet domination in eastern Europe. Britain was allowed dominance of Greece, enabling Britain to control the eastern Mediterranean and the shipping routes to India. Churchill recounted the arrangement thus:

> The moment was apt for business, so I said, 'Let us settle about our affairs in the Balkans ... So far as Britain and Russia are concerned, how would it do for you to have ninety per cent predominance in Roumania, for us to have ninety per cent of the say in Greece, and go fifty-fifty about Yugoslavia?' While this was being translated I wrote out [the proposals] on half a sheet of paper ... I pushed this across to Stalin, who had by then heard the translation. There was a slight pause. Then he took his blue pencil and made a large tick upon it, and passed it back to us. It was all settled in no more time than it takes to set down.[6]

Stalin's concerns were two-fold. First, to create a Soviet sphere of influence as a buffer against any military threat from the west and, second, to assert his dominance over the communist movement internationally – as any emergence of different political orientations there would be likely to find reflection within the Communist Party of the Soviet Union. Tito, however, had just led a successful national liberation struggle, which had unified a fragmented country and introduced a popular socialist revolution.

Tito came into serious conflict with Stalin on three areas of foreign policy. First, Tito contested Yugoslavia's border with Italy. In 1945, the Partisans had entered Trieste. They subsequently withdrew from the city and agreed a demarcation line with Anglo-American forces, but Yugoslavia claimed Trieste as part of its territory. The Soviet leadership was opposed to Yugoslavia's claim. Indeed, as Ulam points out:

> It became known three years later, during the outburst of the Stalin–Tito controversy, that the whole incident created profound irritation in Moscow. Stalin was in the midst of his maneuvers over Poland; he was not going to face a confrontation with the West over a miserable Adriatic port.[7]

Second, Tito wished to forge strong links with neighbouring countries in the Soviet sphere of influence, and proposed a communist Balkan Federation with Bulgaria and Albania, and possibly Greek Macedonia following a hoped-for communist victory in the Greek civil war. Stalin strongly opposed a wider Balkan federation.

Third, Tito actively supported the communist partisans in Greece against the Anglo-US-supported royalist government. Stalin did not, presumably wishing to avoid confrontation with the British. Yugoslavia gave considerable help to the Greek communists, supporting them across their common border, providing a sanctuary from royalist forces as well as a source of supplies. This ceased in 1949, after pro-Tito leaders of the Greek Communist Party were purged by Moscow and the new leadership supported the expulsion of Yugoslavia from the Cominform.

On these and other issues, Tito rejected Stalin's attempt to control Yugoslav foreign policy. The Soviet leadership responded by withdrawing aid, vilifying the Yugoslav leadership and threatening broader intervention. The impact of this split on the other countries of eastern Europe was significant, and in some cases devastating for the communist parties. Tito's assertion of political sovereignty was an attractive approach for many of the communist leaders. This 'national communism', as it became known, was regarded by Stalin as a dangerous deviation which should be stamped out because it would ultimately challenge the monolithic character of the Soviet party itself. Stalin therefore embarked on a series of trials and purges of 'Titoite sympathizers' across eastern Europe. In some cases the top leaderships were removed. In Czechoslovakia, the General Secretary of the Communist Party, Rudolf Slansky, was tried in 1952 and executed, and others like Traicho Kostov in Bulgaria and Laszlo Rajk in Hungary were well-known cases. Rajk's was the first anti-Titoite trial, in 1949 – Foreign Minister of Hungary, he was executed for 'Titoism, treason and espionage for the imperialists'. He was accused of Trotskyist propaganda while a prisoner of war at a camp in Vernet in France, having been captured fighting in the International Brigades during the Spanish Civil War. Within Yugoslavia, Stalin backed a pro-Moscow faction, but never succeeded in seriously challenging Tito. The trials reflected real political differences in the leaderships of the communist parties over the issues of national roads to socialism, which tended to correlate to the war-time experiences of the individuals concerned. Those who had remained in their home countries, leading resistance movements or experiencing fascist prison, were known as 'home' communists and with their own indigenous base of support tended to, in reality or in Stalin's view, greater independence of the Soviet leadership. Those who had spent the war years in Moscow were known as 'Muscovite' communists and tended to favour absolute obedience to the Soviet leadership's line. In spite of the purges, national communism was not stamped out in eastern Europe, and the issue of self-determination within the socialist camp arose over and over again during the post-war period, the suppression of leaderships with real popular support within their countries becoming a significant factor in the eventual loss of support to east European socialist governments.

SELF-MANAGEMENT

Expulsion from the Cominform led to enormous changes in the economic and political life of Yugoslavia. After the Second World War ended, Yugoslavia's rebuilding of foreign trade was largely orientated towards the Soviet Union and eastern Europe, with a whole range of bilateral treaties. This came to an abrupt halt in 1948. Yugoslavia's First Five Year Plan (1947–52) relied on aid and trade with the Soviet Union and Czechoslovakia. The withdrawal of economic support by the Soviet Union made the Plan unworkable in many respects. As Fred Singleton has pointed out: 'As the plan had been based on the assumption of Soviet economic support, it was doomed to fail once Stalin had kicked away its main prop.'[8] Considerable investment had been planned for rapid industrialization, the reconstruction of the infrastructure – particularly for transport and communications, and a huge new building programme for social and cultural facilities. The rift with the Cominform contributed to a massive trade deficit, the loss of certain vital supplies and of manufactured goods, and an increased expenditure on armaments, absorbing desperately scarce resources. The First Five Year Plan still made some striking progress in laying the foundations for rapid industrial development, but Yugoslavia's expulsion from the Soviet bloc necessitated a change in approach to the economy, which was mirrored by political change. In the economy, Tito embarked upon Yugoslavia's famous policy of self-management of enterprises by their workers. The counterpart of this in the political sphere was significant decentralization. Agriculture was one of the first areas where the move away from centralization became apparent – although the government had almost created a massive problem for itself, going through a very rapid full circle to collectivization and back, in the immediate aftermath of expulsion, before fixing on a flexible cooperative-based solution.

Some limited voluntary collectivization had taken place in the early years after the war, so that about 2.4 per cent of land was farmed by peasant work cooperatives, and 3.5 per cent by state farms. In January 1949, however, a drive towards collectivization began, which, while not compulsory, was backed by taxation. This together with a system of compulsory deliveries to the state, was heavily weighted against larger producers. Under this pressure, the number of households in collectives increased broadly seven-fold between 1948 and 1950. However, the collectives turned out to be no more efficient than the private farms, and at the same time considerable peasant resentment developed. By 1951 collectivization had been abandoned for a more peasant-orientated cooperative system. Most peasants left the collectives. Singleton observed that the implementation of collectivization 'almost looked like an attempt to prove Stalin wrong', but it seems more likely that Tito genuinely thought that collectivization would be more productive and would therefore help the newly isolated Yugoslavia not only to meet its food needs but also to release labour for the industrialization process, which was making rapid progress during this period.[9] When it failed to achieve these aims, the policy was changed.

On the political field, tentative steps towards the decentralization of administration had begun earlier. By mid-1949 the People's Committees had been given greater economic and political powers as local government, and there was some devolution of economic powers from federal to republic level. Worker self-management also moved ahead very rapidly. Legislation in 1950 provided for workers' councils to be elected in all industrial enterprises with more than 30 workers. At this stage, the councils were relatively powerless vis-à-vis the managers. However, there was a gradual shift in the balance of power over the subsequent years. During the 1950s workers' councils (in industry and agriculture) and the People's Committees were delegated wider powers.

In 1952 the Communist Party of Yugoslavia was renamed the League of Communists of Yugoslavia. Reforms were introduced to separate it from direct control of the economic and political functions of the state. Tito's intention was to consolidate the departure from administrative command socialism and the name change was symbolic of the breaking from the Soviet-style party. In 1953, the People's Front, the broad electoral bloc created out of AVNOJ, was renamed the Socialist Alliance of the Working People of Yugoslavia (SAWPY), and became primarily engaged in developing self-management at the local electoral level. Real attempts were made during the 1950s to involve people in self-management – the trade unions, for example, provided training courses in self-management as part of an adult education campaign throughout Yugoslavia.[10]

Parallel to these developments, much greater flexibility was introduced into the planning systems, with a move towards general objectives rather than specific targets. In terms of growth of industrial production, the new approach seemed to work: between 1952 and 1959, annual average growth was 13 per cent. However, a key economic problem worsened – that of the foreign trade deficit. As Singleton points out: 'In 1954 97 per cent of the cost of imports was covered by export earnings. In 1961 this had dropped to 62 per cent.'[11] A huge influx of US aid during this period – 61 per cent greater than the value of the deficit – staved off a crisis.

The late 1950s and early 1960s saw further expansion of self-management. The 1957 Labour Relations Act gave the workers' councils greater control over recruitment, dismissal and discipline. Self-management was also extended to education, health, culture and social services. These changes were enshrined in the 1963 constitution, amid talk of the changes being steps towards the ultimate withering away of the state. The new constitution declared Yugoslavia to be a socialist society, renaming the state the Federal Socialist Republic of Yugoslavia. There was considerable ideological debate within the League of Communists, over self-management. Tito took the view that state socialism – along the centralized lines that Yugoslavia had adopted in its first years of post-war development – was a necessary part of the process of building socialism which would then be followed by a more open, democratic and decentralized system. Others such as Milovan Djilas – one of the top Yugoslav leaders who developed the 'new class' theory about bureaucratization in state socialist societies – asserted that the move to self-management came about after the leadership reread Marx after 1948, to try and make sense of what was happening to them in relation to the Cominform crisis. Either way, there can be little doubt that the changes were also driven by the need to retain popular support and allow the economy to function without Soviet support and eventually to enable it to participate more readily in the world market. The extensive economic decentralization of the 1960s was accompanied by the move towards 'market socialism' where worker-managed enterprises would compete with each other with the goal of becoming more efficient and thus more competitive nationally and internationally.

NON-ALIGNMENT

While attempting to build a new domestic social and economic order based on self-management, Yugoslavia performed an adroit balancing act in its external relations. In the early post-war period, Yugoslavia was refused participation in either the western Marshall Plan or the eastern Council for Mutual Economic Assistance (CMEA). In the late 1950s it was given observer status with the

Organization for Economic Cooperation and Development (OECD), the CMEA and the Warsaw Treaty Organization. By the mid-1960s it had met the membership criteria for GATT, and in the 1970s achieved association agreements with the EC and EFTA.

In the early 1960s Tito helped to set up the Non-Aligned Movement, in cooperation with Nehru's India and Nasser's Egypt, as an alternative to the super-power blocs. The Non-Aligned Movement conferences of the 1960s and 1970s discussed the great moral and political issues of the day, and enormously increased Tito's international standing. In the early conferences, in Belgrade in 1961, and Cairo in 1963, nuclear disarmament and colonialism had been the main themes, but by the 1970s, at Lusaka in 1970 and Algiers in 1973, the key issue had become the economic needs of developing countries. In 1967 Yugoslavia, India and Egypt signed an agreement lowering customs duties between their countries which, as Singleton points out, 'was intended to be a model for inter-national trade relations between the countries of the Third World'.[12]

The United States was not particularly happy with Yugoslavia's role in the Non-Aligned Movement and indicated this by periodic cessation of economic support. However, as Susan Woodward has pointed out, the Non-Aligned Movement was actually

> a moderating force against class war at the international level. Yugoslav leaders became leading advocates of peaceful coexistence between ideological camps and of the redistribution of wealth from rich countries to poor in the form of economic assistance (the programme of the new international economic order – NIEO) as a substitute for worldwide communist revolution or direct North-South confrontation.[13]

Yugoslavia had maintained its right to political independence within a socialist orientation at the price of being expelled from the Soviet bloc. It exploited the Cold War to develop economic relations and support from the west, but this constrained its foreign policy with regard to revolutionary or anti-colonial movements. The Non-Aligned Movement earned respect on the moral plane in the Third World but never remotely approached the objective of contributing an alternative pole equivalent to the western and Soviet blocs. This was the lesson that African leaders like Nkrumah learned with the failure of Pan-Africanism in the face of economic imperialism

– they simply did not have the economic and military weight to constitute a real 'third way'.

Yugoslavia attempted to maintain a balance between economic relations with the west, from which it primarily borrowed capital and bought advanced technology, and with the Soviet bloc, with which it exchanged armaments, manufactured goods and construction projects for fuel. Relations with the non-aligned countries could not substitute for these. Trade with the non-aligned group fell during this period, from 17 per cent of Yugoslav foreign trade in 1958, to less than 6 per cent by 1971.[14] Simultaneously, it increased with the west and required Yugoslavia being technologically competitive. As Woodward points out:

> The result was a growing dependence of Yugoslav producers (for both domestic and export markets) on imported technology, spare parts, and trade credit from the West and a persistent trade imbalance. In addition, the short-run solution of loans to finance trade depended on remaining strategically significant to the West.[15]

NATIONS AND CONSTITUTIONS

Constitutionally, Yugoslavia was a multi-national federation comprising the 'nations' of Yugoslavia, the 'nationalities' of Yugoslavia, and other nationalities and ethnic groups. The nations of Yugoslavia were the six officially recognized groups with national homes in one of the federal republics: Serbs, Croats, Slovenes, Montenegrins, Macedonians and Muslims. These last originated as slav converts to Islam under Ottoman rule and were accorded 'nation' status in the 1971 census. These six 'nations' were distinguished from the other nationalities in that they did not have a national homeland outside Yugoslavia. The 'nationalities' of Yugoslavia were ten officially recognized groups: Albanians, Hungarians, Bulgarians, Czechs, Roma, Italians, Romanians, Ruthenians, Slovaks and Turks. With the exception of the Roma and Ruthenians, all these groups had an internationally recognized national homeland outside Yugoslavia. These 'nationalities' had a range of constitutional cultural and language rights. The two largest 'nationalities' were the Albanians in Kosovo, and the Hungarians in Vojvodina, both of which were refused 'nation' status because of the existence of

Albania and Hungary, but accorded autonomous province status within Serbia under the 1974 constitution. Other less numerous nationalities and ethnic groups were Austrians, Greeks, Jews, Germans, Poles, Russians, Ukrainians, Vlachs and others. This category also included those who defined themselves as Yugoslav.[16]

The numerous constitutional changes, from the first constitution in 1946 onwards, are quite revealing about the changes that were taking place within the federal republic, and help to clarify developments during the Tito years. The 1946 constitution instituted a federal structure with a strong central power, legitimized by popular support and the partisan struggle. A bi-cameral legislature comprised a directly-elected Federal Council and a Council of Nationalities, made up of delegates from the assemblies of the republics. These two chambers together, the Federal People's Assembly, elected the Praesidium and the Executive Council. Constitutionally, the Executive was the most powerful body, and Tito was its chairman, as well as being head of the Communist Party. This constitution was modelled on the Soviet constitution of 1936.

In 1953, the constitution was amended – following the split with Moscow – to institutionalize worker self-management. The Federal Council and the Council of Nationalities merged and a Council of Producers was introduced. This reduced the weight of the representation of nationalities, to the advantage of organized workers. This change was hailed as part of an orientation toward the further development of socialism. The 1963 constitution then designated Yugoslavia as 'socialist'. It further developed 'social self-management', giving greater power to communes and republics and self-managing structures within the economy. New indirectly elected chambers were added to the Federal Assembly representing social and economic interests. It was at this point that rotation of office was introduced, the separation of party and state office-holding was introduced for everyone except Tito, and a constitutional court was established.

During the early and mid-1960s, in the context of economic problems, conflict arose within political and economic circles over the scale and pace of reform. Some sought increased reform, blaming persistent statism and centralizing tendencies, particularly 'the strong participation of administrative control in the formation of accumulation and the distribution of investments'.[17] Others favoured putting a rein on the further development of self-management, arguing that it had inflationary propensities and did not necessarily lead to high growth levels. This latter position was defeated during the mid-1960s, particularly with the removal of Alexander Rankovic from power in 1966. From that point, the reform tendency was strengthened, leading to further constitutional changes.

In 1967, the constitution was amended to give more powers to the republics via the strengthening of the Chamber of Nationalities. In 1971, further constitutional amendments considerably increased economic and political decentralization. The right of workers to dispose of the wealth they had created was affirmed, which, as Fred Singleton points out, meant that 'workers' councils were given greater powers in deciding how to allocate the surplus funds of their enterprises between personal incomes, investment, social and welfare funds, and other purposes'.[18] A further amendment guaranteed the right to private enterprise – to own the means of production and to employ workers. Various modifications were made which shifted the balance of power between the republics and the federal government in favour of the former.

However, far from these changes satisfying the aspirations of the reformers and republican interests, as Singleton observes: 'The advance towards autonomy simply whetted the appetite of the more extreme nationalists for further devolution.'[19] It was in Croatia that this tendency found its most vocal form, culminating in a series of protests in November and December 1971. The key issue, which had been bubbling under for some years, was the economic relationship between Zagreb and Belgrade. Croatia was Yugoslavia's biggest foreign currency earner. Under federal regulations, Croatian enterprises could keep only 10 per cent of their foreign currency earnings, the rest being passed to the National Bank in Belgrade. Croatia had previously benefited from substantial amounts of federal investment in its infrastructure to enable the tourist industry to flourish. Now, a nationalist sentiment began to develop on the basis of opposition to what was seen as Croatia subsidizing poorer parts of the federation. There were suggestions that the Croatian nation was being depleted by the number of workers who had work abroad because, it was claimed, their economic future was being squandered on the other republics.

This upsurge of nationalism, primarily based in the developing middle classes, met a harsh response from Tito, himself of Croat nationality, and a purge of the Croat leadership was carried out. In 1972, Tito warned of four emerging threats: one, an excessively centralizing, bureaucratic tendency associated with Rankovic; two, technocrats who favoured concentration of power with managerial elites rather than through self-management; three, nationalists who favoured the concentration of power with the republican elites; and four, liberals attracted by western parliamentarism. Tito suggested that foreign influences were reflected in some of these trends and argued that the aim of all these groups was 'to weaken the system of socialist self-management and to devalue the role of the workers in society'.[20] He concluded that the Communist League should be purified and strengthened and that constitutional changes should be made to ensure that Yugoslavia remained a socialist state.

Tito's 1974 constitution, therefore, sought to stamp out tendencies within the legislative assemblies to function like western parliamentary systems and established a procedure whereby members were delegated by their occupational or interest group and could be recalled if they did not represent their group effectively. The stated intention was to strengthen collective participation and representation and combat individualism – as Crnobrnja observes, 'to reassert the primacy of social(ist) authority as embodied in the "guiding role of the party" and the priority of collective interests over those of the individual economic units'.[21]

The constitution also further decentralized powers to the republics, and went to great lengths to institutionalize equality between them – using quotas and rotation systems to ensure balanced representation, and granting the right of veto over federal legislation to all republics. Tito had argued that the socialist character of Yugoslavia was being eroded, but he did not arrive at an effective solution. Indeed, with hindsight it is possible to see the roots of later problems in this constitution. The locus of power became firmly republican – to the detriment of a Yugoslav identity and national cohesion, and the veto and the necessity for consensus incapacitated decision-making at federal level, rendering it extraordinarily slow. Both of these factors gave rise to considerable difficulties in the 1980s, making it extremely difficult to address the economic problems facing the country and facilitating the re-emergence in a more powerful way of nationalist tendencies in the richest republics orientated against subsidizing the poorest.

The 1974 constitution also accorded Kosovo and Vojvodina virtual republic status within Serbia. As Ramet observes: 'the 1974 federal constitution ... defined the SFRY ... as consisting of eight constituent units, that is, the six republics and two autonomous provinces, thereby granting the provinces a legal status founded not merely on Serbian law, but also on federal law'.[22] There were, for example, eight seats on the Yugoslav federal presidency, with Kosovo and Vojvodina included on the same basis as the nations themselves. This significantly reduced the weight of the largest nation, the Serbs, in the state structure. According to Poulton, the constitutions of Yugoslavia included the 'right to self-determination, including the right to secession' of the nations, but noted that they had united 'on the basis of their will freely expressed' during the Second World War. 'This meant that constitutionally the nations made a binding decision and the right of secession no longer applied.'[23]

REASSERTING COMMUNIST AUTHORITY

Following the purge of the Croatian leadership for nationalism in 1971–2, a wider purge was carried out from the end of 1972 in all the republics. The decentralization of power to the republics and the development of a highly federalized structure had, as Crnobrnja points out, 'the inevitable effect of federalizing the party'.[24] Tito used the purge to try to overcome this within the Communist League and rein in the republican leaders tempted by nationalism.

This process was aimed at strengthening the Communist League and stamping out nationalism and what Tito called 'rotten liberalism' – the latter particularly in Serbia and Slovenia. Tito stated in 1972, about the League: 'In its ranks it needs to have the kind of members and kind of discipline which would prevent the class enemy from taking up positions which, in various forms, he already has in this country.'[25]

Tito had tried to create a constitutional framework which united the south slavs against external domination and did so on the basis of a series of checks and balances designed to accord extensive national rights, thwart separatist tendencies and avoid dominance of the Federation by the largest national group – the Serbs. In this he was remarkably successful by comparison with the pre-war regime. He sustained significant popular support until the end of his life, and the Yugoslav model of self-managed socialism was widely admired. Tito pursued on both domestic and international fields an orientation of balancing between the Soviet Union and the west which succeeded in reconstructing a country devastated by the Second World War. However, as western economic pressure on the country increased and above all growing indebtedness to western financial institutions, the decentralization of political power and elements of marketization within the model of self-managed socialism provided multiple points of leverage for the forces which the western powers were able to utilize to pull the Federation apart after the fall of communism in eastern Europe in 1989.

4

Economic assault: the 1980s and the US drive for a free market

The balance of the Tito years was a delicate one, but it was sustainable while all the elements remained in equilibrium, in particular the room for manoeuvre provided by the Cold War competition between the US and the Soviet Union. The death of Tito in 1980 has often been signalled as a decisive factor in the break-up of Yugoslavia, as though he had kept the republic together by some amazing act of willpower or moral authority. Yet, significant though Tito was, the withdrawal of his person alone could not have fatally fractured Yugoslavia. As Susan Woodward has observed: 'Yugoslav society was not held together by Tito's charisma, political dictatorship, or repression of national sentiments but by a complex balancing act at an international level and an extensive system of rights and overlapping sovereignties.'[1] Greater and more fundamental external factors were at work – first, the leverage which growing indebtedness to western institutions gave over the Yugoslav economy in the 1980s, second, the reintroduction of capitalism into eastern Europe and the dissolution of the Soviet Union at the turn of the decade. Indeed, political change in the Soviet Union during the 1980s had already impacted upon Yugoslavia's position. As Richard Crampton puts it: 'Tito's allegedly neutralist stance in the east–west confrontation was rendered nugatory by Gorbachev's dash for détente.'[2] The first factor resulted in the imposition of increasingly harsh economic pressures on the country, which exacerbated internal divisions. The second factor rendered a non-capitalist Yugoslavia an exception in the region which both the US and Germany, the most powerful state in Europe, now determined to eliminate – though differing in how this should be achieved. The US at first oriented to creating a pro-capitalist federal government, while Germany fostered separatism of Croatia and Slovenia to break up the Federation.

From the early 1980s, Yugoslavia's external balance began to destabilize as US policy towards Yugoslavia began to change. A key

step in this process occurred in 1984, when the Reagan administration targeted the Yugoslav economy in a National Security
Division Directive entitled 'United States Policy Towards
Yugoslavia', the objectives of which 'included "expanded efforts
to promote a 'quiet revolution' to overthrow Communist governments and parties" while re-integrating the countries of eastern
Europe into the orbit of the World market'.[3]

These external pressures keyed into the fault-line of Yugoslavia's
internal situation. IMF-sponsored programmes of liberal macro-
economic reform in the 1980s led to austerity and a deterioration
in living standards. By 1990, industrial production had fallen by 10
per cent and GDP by 7.5 per cent. The terms that were required by
the IMF were designed to secure the privatization and dismantling
of the public sector in Yugoslavia. US Ambassador to Yugoslavia,
Warren Zimmerman, admired the reforms, and 'pointed out that
they became the model that was adopted by Poland and Czechoslovakia'.[4] The economic collapse fuelled increasing tension and
eventual conflict between the republics, as the wealthier republics
were encouraged to hope that outside the Federation they would
gain admission to the German economic zone and the EC. As IMF
pressure mounted, politicians advocating that Croatia and Slovenia
stop subsidizing the poorer parts of the Federation gained ground.

The response to the economic crisis by the Yugoslav federal
government, led from March 1989 by the pro-American Ante
Markovic, was to continue to implement the IMF's austerity
programme. In January 1990 a policy of economic shock therapy
was introduced. The political impact of this was profound, not least
because federal state funding servicing Yugoslavia's debt reduced
the resources available to the republics, thus massively increasing
tensions within the Federation.

External economic pressure was supplemented by political
pressure. In November 1990 the US Congress passed the 1991
Foreign Operations Appropriations Law 101–513, which cut off all
aid, trade, credits and loans from the United States to Yugoslavia
within six months. To qualify for aid to be resumed, each republic
had to conduct elections under State Department supervision of
procedures and results. The legislation also stipulated that only
forces which the State Department defined as 'democratic' would
be allowed funding.[5] In a country that was already highly indebted
and undergoing a brutal austerity programme – leading to unem-

ployment, massive falls in real wages and cuts in subsidies – as the condition for further US loans, this new move by the US could only deepen the political and economic crisis. As Michel Chossudovsky has pointed out: 'The IMF-induced budgetary crisis created an economic "fait accompli" which in part paved the way for Croatia's and Slovenia's formal secession in June 1991.'[6]

ECONOMIC INSTABILITY

At the time of Tito's death in 1980, the Yugoslav economy faced two distinct but interrelated problems: domestic structural weaknesses, and the knock-on effects of global economic crisis. Domestically the economy was hampered by insufficient production of raw materials and industrial inputs, which meant that Yugoslavia was highly reliant on imports to facilitate industrial growth. This contributed to the massive balance-of-payments deficit, and necessitated import substitution – but this in itself required further loans to develop the industry to extract the raw materials and produce the inputs. The impact of the increase in oil prices in the 1970s was enormous for Yugoslavia, as she was faced with increased bills for her oil imports, partially offset as she began to develop her domestic coal and hydro-electric resources. Nevertheless, the oil-price crisis severely exacerbated Yugoslavia's massive balance-of-payments deficit problem. As Singleton and Carter observed in the early 1980s: 'As the western economies stagnate, they become more resistant to the pleas of the Yugoslavs that they allow them to export more of their goods in order to pay for the imports necessary to sustain the momentum of industrial growth.'[7] The Poles were also badly hit by the economic recession, for their economic recovery strategy had been founded on export-oriented industrialization, heavily funded by western loans. As their goods came on-stream, the projected western markets for them collapsed. As a result, the debt crisis mounted.

The rise in international interest rates in the early 1980s worsened this problem. As Aldcroft and Morewood point out, Yugoslavia, which by 1979 had a deficit on its current account of $3.7 billion and by 1980 a foreign debt of $18 billion, 'had become danger-ously vulnerable to variable-interest "roll-over" loans from the private sector and by 1981 was paying an average rate of interest of no less than 18.7 per cent on its debts, a far cry from the 7.3 per cent of 1972'.[8] A further blow was the drying-up of demand for Yugoslav labour within the west European economies. Hundreds of thousands of workers returned to Yugoslavia, simultaneously exacerbating the problem of unemployment and reducing by half the remittances which had 'financed half the Yugoslav trade deficit since the early 1960s'.[9]

Austerity measures were first introduced by the Yugoslav federal government in 1979 in an attempt to cut down domestic consumption of imports and increase exports, but the balance of payments was not noticeably improved. The government was forced to turn to the IMF for a loan, which was granted. The IMF made a further loan in 1982, on condition of domestic reform, 'an anti-inflationary macro-economic stabilization policy of radical austerity, trade and price liberalization, and institutional reforms to impose on firms and governments monetary discipline and real price incentives'.[10] In July 1981 the federal government formed an economic commission to address the crisis. Known as the Kraigher Commission for the Reform of the Economic System, it was headed by the federal president, the Slovene, Sergej Kraigher, and comprised representatives from the republics and autonomous provinces. Functioning for two years, the Commission eventually published its conclusions in 1983 under the title, *Long-term Programme of Economic Stabilization*. It recommended the retention of the basic structure of the economy and social ownership, but with the introduction of increased market elements and the liberalization of trade. This was the result of a compromise between those who supported the fundamentals of self-managing socialism, and those who wanted more market-oriented reforms.

These discussions in the early 1980s about the nature and extent of economic reform, which focused around the Kraigher Commission, also – given the integrated relationship of political and economic self-management – raised the issue of political reform. In 1985, the Vrhovec Commission was convened, to assess the need for change in the political system, possible modifications to the constitution of 1974, and the linking of political and economic reform. In 1986, it published *Critical Analysis of the Functioning of the Political System*. The two commissions differed considerably in their overall approach to reform. As Ivo Bicanic observes: 'Each of the reports represents a different and mutually exclusive vision' over a range of key issues, including markets, factor costs, the role of money and finance, and the enterprise, 'the former stressing the enterprise and the latter its constituent parts, that is, the basic organisation of associated labour ... Thus to a great extent the *Critical Analysis* implied a return from markets to the Associated Labour Paradigm.'[11]

The basic conflict in the federal leadership at this time was over whether reform should aim to regenerate self-managing socialism or to create a market economy. The pro-market reformers echoed the advice of the IMF to encourage market-oriented reform, open up the economy and to break down the government's tightening control of investment. Yugoslavia's main creditor nations – including the US – 'reprogrammed the government component of [Yugoslavia's debt] and provided a political justification for the commercial banks to refinance the commercial component of the debt'. As Crnobrnja points out: 'The understanding was that Yugoslavia should use this political and financial credit to con-solidate the situation at home, but primarily through market-oriented reforms.'[12]

The impact of market-oriented reforms on the population was severe. Food subsidies were ended in 1982 and the cost of essentials such as petrol, fuel, food and transport rose by a third in the following year. Rationing was introduced for petrol, electricity, sugar and flour. A ban was put on all imports not required for the productive process. New investment in social services and public infrastructure was suspended. Between 1979 and 1985 the value of the Yugoslav currency fell by 90 per cent, largely due to two devaluations. Unemployment rapidly accelerated, particularly amongst the young and in urban areas, as loss-making firms were required to make workers redundant. Inflation rose rapidly, incomes dropped sharply, and savings were depleted for 80 per cent of households. As Woodward observes:

> As early as 1983 the government acknowledged a deep depression. Gross domestic product fell 1.3 percent in 1983, and average capacity utilization in industry was below 70 percent ... By the end of 1984 the average income was approximately 70 percent of the official minimum for a family of four, and the population living below the poverty line increased from 17 to 25 percent.[13]

The dissatisfaction of the workforce was demonstrated by an 80 per cent increase in industrial action from 1982 to 1983.

The IMF reform programme of the early 1980s also involved a shift of emphasis within the economy, towards production for western markets, which favoured those sectors and areas with closer links to the west. There was also a move away from primary production for export towards manufactured export production. Both of these factors favoured certain republics over others:

> Slovenia and large areas of Croatia had a significant advantage, and Serbia somewhat less; demand declined for producers in agriculture, mining and metallurgy, and defense, which tended to concentrate in Bosnia and Hercegovina, Macedonia, and Serbia proper and its two provinces, Kosovo and Vojvodina.[14]

In 1989, the federal government introduced legislation to enforce and support a transition to a market economy via the 1990 IMF/World Bank reform programme, 'largely masterminded', according to Ivo Bicanic, 'by the American economist J. Sachs'.[15] The Enterprise Law, required by the country's creditors to speed the breakdown of social ownership and self-management, abolished self-managed, socially-owned enterprises, replacing them with private enterprises managed by owners and creditors. The Banking Law dismantled over 50 per cent of the country's socially owned banks. With credit to the industrial sector frozen, the Financial Operations Act allowed enterprises that were insolvent for 30 days to be taken over by their creditors. This procedure catapulted many enterprises into bankruptcy, leading to the redundancy of over 600,000 workers, largely concentrated in Serbia, Macedonia, Kosovo and Bosnia-Hercegovina. Trade was deregulated, leading to a flood of imports, negatively affecting domestic producers.

In September 1990 the World Bank estimated that over 2,500 further enterprises were bankrupt. As Chossudovsky points out:

> Bearing in mind that 600,000 workers had already been laid off by bankrupt firms prior to September 1990, these figures suggest that some 1.9 million workers (out of a total of 2.7 million) had been classified as 'redundant'. The 'insolvent' firms concentrated in the energy, heavy industry, metal processing, forestry and textiles sectors were among the largest industrial enterprises in the country representing (in September 1990) 49.7% of the total (remaining and employed) industrial work-force.[16]

The reform package and its supporting legislation were designed to bring about the fastest possible dismantling and privatization of the socialized Yugoslav economy. The chaos, fragmentation and despair that it brought to Yugoslavia was comparable to what happened in Russia as a result of the 1992 IMF-sponsored reform programme.

POLITICAL INSTABILITY

The IMF-led economic reform policies carried out by the federal government during the early 1980s, under the leadership of Milka Planinc, required a recentralization of economic policy and control. As Woodward points out:

> the restrictive monetary, fiscal, and foreign trade policies also required a fundamental change in political authority over economic assets ... In contrast to the extreme territorial decentralization of the 1970s, these emergency policies required federal assertion of economic authority over the republics, leaving little room for negotiation.[17]

For example, the National Bank in Belgrade regained control over foreign exchange operations, having distributed responsibility for this to the republics only five years earlier. IMF advisers were strongly in favour of increased federal control to facilitate more rapid decision-making and effective policy implementation. The long process required for consultation and consensus-reaching under the devolved system was perceived to be an obstacle to reform.

Recentralization was strongly opposed for a number of reasons. The wealthier republics were concerned about the loss of economic control, whereas the poorer republics were worried about loss of political control and control of local assets. The issue of redistribution of wealth within the federation was a fundamental one. From the perspective of the anti-federalists in Croatia and Slovenia, 'the economic crisis was the result of inappropriate investment choices, waste of funds transferred as aid or subsidies to poorer republican or provincial governments, and politically influenced choices by monetary authorities'.[18] As the economic crisis worsened throughout the 1980s, so this argument gained strength, and those defending decentralization over IMF-led recentralization increasingly argued for reducing the political and economic role of the federal government. The ultimate logic of this was the drive for independence by the richest two republics that felt they were suffering most from the economic measures and subsidizing the rest of Yugoslavia – spearheaded by Slovenia and followed by Croatia. As Benson observes:

> As the mounting economic crisis began to put paid to years of rising prosperity based on separate development, Slovenian separatism took an anti-Yugoslav turn. The Slovenes emerged as relentless critics of all federal institutions, and as advocates of confederal arrangements in which Slovenia would have a privileged place.[19]

In June 1985, the Slovenian and Croatian parliaments rejected three laws on the recentralization of foreign economic relations. They also opposed the introduction of majority rather than consensus decision-making into federal structures – a change sought by foreign creditors to increase efficiency and speed up the reform process. Slovenia's economy was already well integrated with western economies and she did not favour greater reintegration into the Yugoslav market – on the contrary, she favoured an increasing western orientation. Croatia's leadership was opposed to recentralization and what it saw as continued subsidy, at Croatia's expense, of the poorer regions of the federation.

The situation in Serbia differed considerably from that in Slovenia and Croatia, both economically and politically. On the economic front, Serbia had fallen below the Yugoslav average in the 1970s, had an increasing unemployment problem, and was facing problems of internal migration as a result of tensions in the autonomous province of Kosovo and the economic reforms. Politically, the republic's leadership favoured economic recentralization on IMF lines, the reintegration of the Yugoslav market, and reassertion of Belgrade's control over the autonomous provinces of Kosovo and Vojvodina which had been devolved under the constitution of 1974, including control over investment and budgets. The autonomous provinces' governments had power of veto over Belgrade's policy for the whole of Serbia, while the reverse was not true for Serbia itself. Serbia's leaders did not consider that this situation led to effective government.[20]

This conflict – between a recentralizing federal government pushing IMF liberal reform, and two pro-market republican gov-

ernments seeking greater independence with an ultimate perspective of separatism, led to the increasing use of nationalist arguments
by the republican leaderships to win their case. With the opening-
up of the electoral system to multi-party elections in 1990, this was
used to their advantage with the voters.

THE QUESTION OF KOSOVO

An issue which was much exacerbated by the economic crisis of the
1980s was that of the autonomous province of Kosovo. The
majority of the population of Kosovo were ethnically Albanian,
defined constitutionally as a 'nationality' of Yugoslavia – as a state
of Albania exists outside Yugoslavia – and therefore not entitled to
full republican status within Yugoslavia. In 1981 Albanians in
Yugoslavia as a whole numbered around 1.7 million, or 7.7 per
cent of the Yugoslav population. The majority of the Albanian
population was concentrated in Kosovo, where they made up
around 85 per cent of the population. Other large Albanian communities lived in western Macedonia, where they comprised around
20 per cent of the population, and also in Montenegro and southern
Serbia proper.

Kosovo is a powerful symbol in Serbian history, forming the
heart of the mediaeval kingdom of Serbia, and it houses many of
the great historic monuments of the Orthodox Church. It has,
however, also been of significance to the development of Albanian
national identity: the founding of the League of Prizren in Kosovo
in 1878 marked the beginning of the Albanian national revival.
The impetus for the creation of an Albanian national state was
relatively limited, however, as there were no obstacles to advancement for Muslim Albanians within the Ottoman Empire. Indeed
as Hugh Poulton points out: 'It can be argued that the Albanian
national revival was in many ways a reaction to Serb and Greek
claims on the decaying Ottoman Empire.'[21] The state of Albania
was created in 1912 during the break-down of the Ottoman Empire
in the Balkan Wars, with the primary impetus for this, according
to Poulton, coming from the Great Powers, 'notably Austria-
Hungary who viewed the expansion of the new Balkan states,
especially Serbia, with great alarm'.[22]

However, the pre-existence of newly-won Balkan states meant
that some areas with large Albanian majorities were already included

in other countries where they constituted national minorities. After the First World War a process of settlement and emigration began in Kosovo, with the Yugoslav government encouraging Serbian and Montenegrin settlement and Albanian emigration. This process, together with political, cultural and linguistic domination, alienated the Albanian population, and many welcomed the forcible break-up of Yugoslavia during the Second World War, supporting the inclusion of Albanian populated areas into the Italian-sponsored Kingdom of Albania. The previous territorial settlement was restored after the Second World War, although Tito did not allow the re-settlement of the considerable number of Serbs who had been pushed out of Kosovo during the war.

The status of Albanians within Yugoslavia improved under communist rule, with recognition as a distinct national group, their language recognized as one of Yugoslavia's official languages, and the right to education in that language. Nationalist activity continued, however, to a greater or lesser extent throughout the whole post-war period. While many Albanians in Yugoslavia were satisfied with the political settlement, others favoured republican status for Kosovo within Yugoslavia. Some saw republican status as a step on the way to a Greater Albania, pulling all Albanian occupied regions outside Albania into a unified nation state.

Such an aim was never countenanced by the Yugoslav leadership, since it would have meant the breaking away of significant parts of three of the Yugoslav federal republics. Indeed, the constitutional limitation on nationalities with states outside Yugoslavia was designed to forestall a dynamic of nationalities like the Albanians and Hungarians first forming republics then seceding to merge with Albania and Hungary. However, the federal leadership did make real efforts to meet the aspirations of the Kosovan Albanians, within the existing republican and territorial framework. In 1968, as the demand for republican status became very vocal, new constitutional amendments were introduced to give Kosovo increased status – short of a republic. An Albanian language university was established in Pristina, and it was permitted to fly the Albanian flag. The constitution of 1974 consolidated this further, granting Kosovo status as a constituent member of the federation, thus entitling it to a vote on the presidency and other bodies, equal to full republics. The 1970s were a period of advance for the Kosovan Albanians, who comprised over two-thirds of the membership of both the provincial communist league and police by the end of the decade. However, in economic terms, Kosovo remained extremely under-developed. Unemployment was three times the federal average and most Kosovan Albanians worked in the agricultural sector on family smallholdings. Industrially, the province had a strong mining sector – including the massive Trepca mines, which employed 19,000 – producing coal and minerals, and related metallurgical industry and electricity production. However, as Benson points out, these industries 'were capital-intensive and generated few jobs'.[23] The severity of the unemployment problem turned many young people towards higher education at Pristina University as a means of advancement, but as Poulton observes, this

> helped create a large Albanian intelligentsia with little outlet in terms of job opportunities for them; in 1984 unemployment in Kosovo was 29.1% compared to 12.7% national average and only 1.8% in Slovenia. In addition in Kosovo, 70% of those unemployed were aged 25 years or under.[24]

In the mid-1970s, a number of leading Kosovan Albanian nation-alists were arrested and imprisoned, and they were accused of organizing against the state, and of 'crimes endangering the terri-torial integrity and independence of Yugoslavia'.[25] One of their number, Adem Demaqi, was accused of founding the National Liberation Movement of Kosovo, which had the aim of uniting Kosovo with Albania. With hindsight one can see that the Yugoslav government was faced with a very real problem, where serious and genuine issues and grievances – like regional economic disparities and unemployment – provided fertile ground for nationalist extremists. On the other hand, with higher living standards than Albania as a result of the federal system of redistribution of wealth which benefited Kosovo, there was also a powerful economic basis for the pro-Yugoslav Albanian trends in Kosovo. It was the under-mining of this economic mechanism by marketization and the drive by Croatia and Slovenia against subsidizing the poorer parts of the Federation which undid this economic integrating mechanism and fuelled increasing national divisions. Nationalist activity intensified during the late 1970s and came to a head in the spring of 1981, when major demonstrations took place in Pristina and other parts of Kosovo, demanding republican status, and in some cases union with Albania. Following violent clashes with the police, a State of Emergency was declared, the army entered Kosovo, and around 2,000 people were arrested. By the end of 1983, 658 convictions were made for 'irredentist' activity (aiming to join Albania).[26] It was apparent that there was a huge proliferation of nationalist groups in Kosovo at this time, and with the failure of the 1981 protests to move republican status nearer, some of them began to turn towards violent means to achieve their ends and a number of arrests were made in 1984 for arms smuggling and causing explosions. Such groups, as Poulton points out, 'using or advocating violence, were, however, a minority'.[27] This has, in fact, always been the case in Kosovo, even in the elections in Kosovo after the NATO bombing of Yugoslavia in 1999, the party of the Kosovo Liberation Army was defeated by Ibrahim Rugova's peaceful Democratic League of Kosovo.

Repression of nationalist sentiment and organization took place throughout the 1980s, in some cases affecting people's employment, and in the course of the decade, in the region of 7,000 Kosovan Albanians were imprisoned for nationalist activity. However, in other respects, including culturally, the Kosovan Albanians had a full range of rights: Albanian was an official language, and there were Albanian language newspapers, television and radio. Indeed, Kosovan Albanians predominated in all public sectors, including the Communist League, police and courts, and so the conflict within Kosovo at this point was between Albanians – those nationalists in court would be tried by Albanians in the Albanian language.[28] As Poulton says: 'These "official" Albanians (often referred to by demonstrators as "traitors" of whom, perhaps Rahman Morina, the Kosovo League of Communists leader who died in 1990, was the most renowned) were defending the status quo – i.e. the communist system and the 1974 Constitution.'[29] The Kosovan Albanians were themselves divided about the political structure, nature and future of Kosovo.

As the economic crisis deepened, relations between the Albanian and Serb inhabitants of Kosovo deteriorated as competition for jobs and resources increased. There was widespread Serbian emigration from Kosovo during the 1980s, and accusations from the émigrés that they had experienced intimidation and even attack from Kosovan Albanians. Crnobrnja observes: 'Albanian nationalists were applying overt and covert pressure on the Serbs and Montenegrins to move out of Kosovo, with the purpose of making it ever more ethnically homogeneous.'[30] Indeed, Norah Beloff has described this push for an Albanian-only Kosovo by sections of the Kosovan Albanian community as ethnic cleansing.[31]

In this context, Kosovo began to feature more prominently in Serbian politics and became a focus for Serbian national feeling at a time when the population was being severely stretched through the economic crisis. In October 1986, a memorandum from the Serbian Academy of Sciences and Arts appeared in the press, expressing Serbian resentment about the situation facing the republic. As well as objecting to the division of Serbia into three parts, the memo spoke strongly about the situation in Kosovo:

> 'The physical, political, legal, cultural genocide of the Serb population of Kosovo and Metohija is the greatest defeat of the freedom struggles Serbia has waged from Orasac 1804 to the 1941 rising,' claiming that 200,000 Serbs had left the province during the previous 20 years.[32]

Indeed, whereas the population of Kosovo had been 50 per cent Serb at the beginning of the Second World War, by the late 1980s it had reduced to around 10 per cent. They criticized Tito for promoting every nation but the Serbs.

By 1987 60,000 Kosovan Serbs had signed a petition, asserting that genocide was taking place against the Serbs in Kosovo. The constitutional balance within Serbia also became a source of considerable resentment in Serbia. While Serbian laws had to go to the provincial parliaments in Vojvodina and Kosovo for confirmation, the reverse was not the case. Thus, a situation existed, as Crnobrnja points out, 'in which the provinces could block Serbia's passage of laws for the entire territory but Serbia could not block its own autonomous provinces on their territory, though they were nominally a part of the republic'.[33] Constitutional change which the Serbian government might wish to introduce was subject to veto by the two autonomous provinces of Vojvodina and Kosovo. During the mid-1980s Serbia discussed this perceived inequality at every level of province, republic and federation, but did not make any headway in resolving this matter.

MILOSEVIC

At a time when Yugoslavia was near breaking point with massive external debt, huge unemployment, the economic sufferings introduced by IMF austerity programmes, contradictory class pressures within the Communist League at federal and republican level, a new leadership was consolidated within the Serbian Communist League. In 1986 Slobodan Milosevic became Chairman of the Serbian League of Communists. He was relatively young, at the age of 46, for high political office, and came from a primarily economic background. In the 1960s he had served as economic advisor to the mayor of Belgrade, and had become Director of the state Tehnogas company in 1973. In 1978 he went to work for the Beobanka financial institution, where he built up international contacts particularly, according to Robert Thomas, with America. However, his economic position was for the reform of self-management rather than its abolition, and he 'stressed that "the chief fundamental form of property under socialism remains social property"'.[34] This position, combined with his lack of enthusiasm for liberal democracy, clearly put him at odds with western institutions, which were primarily concerned after 1989 with the integration of the former state socialist countries into their own political, economic and military institutional framework. The demonization of Milosevic was eventually to know no bounds, far outstripping the attacks and criticisms of leaders that could be considered responsible for, or to have condoned, similar terrible and tragic events, such as Tudjman or Izetbegovic. In 1995, former US Ambassador to Yugoslavia, Warren Zimmerman, described Milosevic in the following way:

> His manner is affable and displays his light side. Unfortunately, the man is almost totally dominated by his dark side ... He is a man of extraordinary coldness. I never saw him moved by an individual case of human suffering; for him, people are groups (Serbs, Muslims) or simply abstractions. Nor did I ever hear him say a charitable or generous word about any human being, not even a Serb. This chilling personality trait made it possible for Milosevic to condone, encourage, and even organize the unspeakable atrocities committed by Serbian citizens in the Bosnian war. It also accounts for his habitual mendacity, as in his outrageous distortion of Serbian behaviour in Kosovo. For Milosevic, truth has only a relative value. If it serves his objectives, it is employed; if not, it can be discarded.[35]

Louis Sell reported that 'one of the few constants in Milosevic's personality is mendacity', and said that US psychiatrists who have apparently studied Milosevic closely consider him to have a 'malignant narcissistic' personality and to believe his own lies.[36] It is, of course, possible that Milosevic had a different analysis and understanding of what was going on in Yugoslavia. Zimmerman, for example, argues that Serbian claims with regard to Serbian occupied areas outside the republic of Serbia had no consistent principles behind them. This was, of course, incorrect, because all Serbian claims were based on their rights under the Yugoslav constitution.[37]

In the same article as his rather unscientific personality analysis of Milosevic, Zimmerman also comments on Tudjman, observing that, unlike Milosevic who is motivated by power, he is obsessed with nationalism, has overseen serious violations of the rights of Serbs, and has denigrated the Holocaust; but, Zimmerman observes: 'Tudjman's saving grace, which distinguishes him from Milosevic, is that he really wants to be a western statesman. He therefore listens to Western expressions of concern and criticism and often does something about them.'[38] In some senses, Zimmerman has hit upon the core of the issue. Tudjman could be backed because he was essentially pro-western, whereas Milosevic had to be broken, because he was not.

Milosevic rapidly became hugely popular. In April 1987, Milosevic addressed a rally on the historic Kosovo battlefield, declaring – with reference to the perceived ill-treatment of Serbs by Albanians – 'No-one should be allowed to beat you!' This won Milosevic huge support from a population that was under great strain and feeling increasingly angry. Milosevic subsequently replaced Ivan Stambolic as President of Serbia, winning 'the anti-bureaucratic revolution' inside the communist establishment, and successfully leading a campaign against what he considered to be excessive liberalism within the Serbian league – especially in Belgrade. He accused Stambolic and his supporters of 'being too lenient on Albanians in Kosovo and of failing to protect Serbian territorial integrity and Serbs and Montenegrins from forced expulsion'.[39]

Milosevic's championing of the Serbian cause against the autonomous provinces was in a sense 'saying what had for long been unsayable under the prohibitions of the Titoist state. The political inconsistencies of the constitution served as an easily iden-tifiable "cause" for the multiplicity of ills afflicting post-Tito

Serbia.'[40] Thus, the terrible impact of the IMF reforms, which had exacerbated and compounded the tendencies towards secessionism in Slovenia and Croatia, also contributed to the rise of Serbian nationalism. Milosevic won considerable popular support through his articulation of Serbian resentment, particularly over the constitutional situation and the position of Serbs in Kosovo and he mobilized this support effectively, to bring about changes in the republican leadership in line with his own political perspective. He attempted, perhaps successfully, to achieve what Robert Thomas has described as 'a populist crusade in which he sought to establish a link between himself and the population transcending normal institutional politics'.[41] It is notable, however, that whilst Milosevic clearly sought to redress what many Serbs felt to be the wrongs towards the Serbs in Kosovo and towards the Serbian republic with regard to the constitutional issue, he also argued for the unity and equality of citizens on a non-national basis. For example, in his speech at Kosovo Field in June 1989, which has often been portrayed as nationalist rabble-rousing, he stated:

> Serbia has never had only Serbs living in it. Today, more than in the past, members of other peoples and nationalities also live in it. This is not a disadvantage for Serbia. I am truly convinced that it is its advantage. National composition of almost all countries in the world today, particularly developed ones, has also been changing in this direction. Citizens of different nationalities, religions and races have been living together more and more frequently and successfully. Socialism in particular, being a progressive and just democratic society, should not allow people to be divided in the national and religious aspect. The only differences one can and should allow in socialism are between hard working people and idlers and between honest people and dishonest people. Therefore, all people in Serbia who live from their own work, honestly, respecting other people and other nations, are in their own republic.[42]

Milosevic succeeded in building an extremely broad coalition of support across Serbian society – that was pro-Yugoslav but against the perceived anti-Serb bias of Tito's constitutions, that was for the protection of Serbs, and that was for the defence of those suffering under the economic reforms. Thus, he was able, with the exception of the liberals, to unite the vast majority of Serbian society, including the increasing numbers of socially and economically marginalized elements, created by the liberalizing economic reforms. Through this mass movement, 'the happening of the people', he achieved a kind of 'supra-political' status[43] which he maintained amongst many for the whole of his political career.

5
Crisis response

The federal republics responded to the crisis of the 1980s in different ways. In the two richest republics, Slovenia and Croatia, political forces that stood for the deepening of free-market policies had come to the fore. However, while one might assume that this would have made them favourable to the IMF-inspired policies coming from the federal government in Belgrade, this was not the case. They were deeply opposed to the recentralization demanded by the IMF and were more interested in the possibilities of rapid integration into the German and Austrian economic zone on their northern borders. Notwithstanding the liberal market elements of the IMF reform of the federal government, they began to pursue secession from Yugoslavia in order no longer to have to subsidize the poorer parts of the federation or conform to foreign exchange retention quotas and other policies which they considered inimical to their economic interests. In Serbia, on the other hand, there was simultaneously a powerful reaction from some sections of the community against the liberal market policies of the federal government – including massive strikes by hundreds of thousands of workers against the austerity programme – and a positive attitude towards the IMF recentralization policy which was perceived to be in Serbia's economic interests. There was mounting anger within Serbia about the perceived ill-treatment of Serbs within Kosovo, and the unequal constitutional balance within Serbia. At that time, while Serbs made up the largest proportion of the federation's population, they had one-eighth of the federal presidency, made up of the six republics and the two autonomous regions within Serbia of Vojvodina and Kosovo. Milosevic led a campaign to redress these perceived injustices, which found a real popular echo not least because many people were suffering real hardship as a result of the drastic effect on living standards of the federal government's economic policy, and this gave an outlet for their grievances. This led to a new Serbian constitution in September 1990, which effectively removed the autonomous status of the two regions, although it did identify Serbia as the state of all those living in it, as opposed to the constituting of citizenship on a national basis which was to cause so many problems in Croatia. Serbia thus gained control of three seats on the Presidency which, together with their allies Montenegro, would give them four out of eight seats in their struggle to maintain the federation, defend the constitutional position of the Serbs, and oppose the scale and pace of the neo-liberal IMF economic reforms which were having such a devastating impact on the country.

This development, when combined with the clampdown on Albanian nationalism and secessionism within Kosovo, led to accusations of extreme nationalism against Slobodan Milosevic. Considerable hostility to Serbian policies was expressed by some of the other republican leaderships, and once multi-party democracy had been introduced and the monopoly of the Communist League had ended, this provided a pretext for the anti-communist nationalist parties in Slovenia and Croatia to intensify their campaigns to break away from Yugoslavia. Milosevic was accused of having plans for a 'Greater Serbia', but as Norah Beloff points out: 'In reality, as any study of events in Belgrade will confirm, the Serb leader never used the words "Greater Serbia", except to refute accusations made by outside powers.'[1] In fact, the real danger lay with the development of an exclusive ethnic nationalism in Croatia, which asserted 'Croatia for the Croats' and stripped the large Serbian communities of their constitutional rights. The drive for an ethnic-based republic in Croatia was inevitably going to lead to conflict with Serbia, in defence of the rights – even lives – of the Krajina Serbs. A multi-national, secular and federal Yugoslavia was the only real way to ensure security for all, but this had been so eroded by secessionism, and the federal leadership so weakened by the disastrous impact of the economic reforms – and the JNA prohibited by the EU from acting to defend Yugoslavia – that in the end the Serb leadership fought primarily to defend Serbs in other republics where their rights were under threat.

The first multi-party elections in the republics took place in 1990, with nationalist parties coming to power in Croatia and Slovenia, although overall throughout the federation there was a considerable base of support for communist and former communist parties. Serbia returned the Socialist Party leader Slobodan Milosevic (the Socialist Party was formed from the Serbian section of the Yugoslav League of Communists merged with its linked mass organization) as president. The republic of Montenegro elected a communist president, and like Serbia, decided that they did not wish to take the path of rapid economic liberalization and orientation to the west and that they wished to remain within a federal republic of Yugoslavia. Thus Yugoslavia was politically divided both between and within republics.

In June 1991, Slovenia and Croatia decided that the solution was to leave Yugoslavia. They proclaimed their independence from the federal republic and orientated themselves towards the west, to be followed in September 1991 by Macedonia. A different approach, however, was taken by Serbia. In December 1991, Germany began the re-Balkanization of the country, and recognized Croatian and Slovenian independence. It forced the EC to do the same in January 1992 – even though Croatia's minority rights provision did not meet the EU's own criteria – by refusing to support the Maastricht Treaty unless the EC recognized the secessionist states. Bosnia-Hercegovina declared its independence in March 1992 and was recognized by the EC and the US in April 1992. In April 1992, the two republics of Serbia and Montenegro constituted the new Federal Republic of Yugoslavia.

POLITICAL CHANGE IN SLOVENIA

A crucial tension that became increasingly clear in the late 1980s was that between Slovenia and Serbia. Slovenia's orientation was towards greater autonomy within Yugoslavia and greater decentralization of powers, whereas Serbia's was towards a greater centralization within the federation and a rebalancing of the constitution to redress what it considered to be an anti-Serb emphasis. This difference in orientation brought the two republics increasingly into conflict. From the mid-1980s there had been a developing movement for increased liberal democratic freedoms – and ultimately, for multi-party democracy – in Slovenia, and also a tendency towards loosening the bonds of federalism. The origins of both of these were ostensibly in the Slovenian youth organization. They argued for increased freedom of speech and assembly, and the popularity of this demand grew among university students, who engaged in protest around environmental protection issues. They also challenged the Titoite ideal by refusing to participate, in 1986, in the traditional annual youth relay, which symbolized the unity of the youth of Yugoslavia. As Crnobrnja observes: 'This tradition, continued even after Tito's death, symbolized probably more than anything else the continuity of Tito's Yugoslavia.'[2] The Slovenian leadership, while not officially supporting the youth organization's position, did nevertheless condone the withdrawal, but they were completely isolated in this decision - no other republican leadership supported them, as it was seen as a direct attack on Titoite Yugoslavia.

The Slovenian youth organization then launched an attack on the credibility of the JNA, via its journal, *Mladina*, accusing the army leadership of extravagance and corruption and calling in 1987, 'for legal reforms permitting independent social movements and recognition of conscientious objector status and a civilian national service option for draftees'.[3] However, the decision of federal army officials to prosecute the editor of *Mladina* for treason without the knowledge of the Slovenian political leadership served to unify the republic against the federal authorities. As a result, a Committee for the Defence of Human Rights was set up, which rapidly attracted over 100,000 members. As Seroka points out, this was the first mass organization in Yugoslavia outside the control of the Communist League. This was followed in January 1989 by the formation of the Slovenian Democratic Alliance, which campaigned for multi-party democracy. By the middle of 1989 a wide range of political organizations had been formed, from diverse political perspectives, but all supporting the Slovenian leadership against other republican leaderships, and all urging more autonomy for Slovenia within the federation. In August 1989, Slovenia ratified a constitution, which gave itself the right to secede from Yugoslavia and nullify federal laws, and it was eventually agreed that multi-party elections should be held early in 1990. This step had the support of the Slovenian communist leadership, which argued in the federation for a multi-party system, but it was not otherwise the case that republican communist leaderships supported pluralist political reform and their attempts came to nothing. Indeed, tensions between the republican communist leaderships increased during the late 1980s, not only regarding economic arrangements, but also over the constitutional changes in Serbia and Serbia's Kosovo policy. Slovenia was critical of the latter; indeed, according to Crnobrnja, the Slovene leadership 'openly and actively backed the Albanian leadership of Kosovo',[4] being outspoken in their support of the miners' strike at Stari Trg, which demanded the independence of Kosovo from Serbia. There was an attempt by the Serbs to hold a 'rally for truth' in Ljubljana to inform the Slovenes of the reality of life for Serbs in Kosovo, but they were told by the Slovenian government that they would be turned away at the borders of Slovenia, so the rally was never held. Similar rallies were, however, held in Serbian communities in the Krajina and in Bosnian Serb regions. The result of this Slovene/Serb confrontation over Kosovo was the declaration of a Serbian economic boycott of Slovenia. In response, the Slovenes sent their share of inputs into the federal fund for underdeveloped regions directly to Kosovo, ignoring the constitutional change, which meant that it should have gone via Belgrade.[5]

The Croatian communist leadership did not openly take sides in this increasing hostility between Slovenia and Serbia; indeed, their position was described at the time as the 'Croatian silence'.[6] The Croatian communist leadership, under Stipe Suvar, favoured a moderate stance, including offering greater autonomy to the Serbs in Croatia at the same time as Croatia received greater autonomy within Yugoslavia. However, while Suvar was pursuing this line, a strongly nationalistic position was being developed and promoted by Franjo Tudjman. Tudjman had been a Partisan fighter during the Second World War, and subsequently an officer in the JNA, but had, as Benson describes, been 'reincarnated' as a nationalist historian in the 1960s. In 1980 he published a book arguing that Bosnia-Hercegovina was 'by historical right and geographical logic an integral part of Croatia'[7] and was imprisoned for 'maliciously misrepresenting Yugoslavia abroad'. Tudjman also achieved notoriety for his writings which belittled the tragedy and criminal nature of the Holocaust. Nevertheless, Tudjman's extreme nationalist views won him considerable support within Croatia in the context of the economic crisis and the social instability of the 1980s, which exacerbated tensions between the republics. As Warren Zimmerman observed: 'For better or worse, Croatian nationalism is defined by Tudjman – intolerant, anti-Serb, and authoritarian. These attributes – together with an aura of wartime fascism, which Tudjman has done nothing to dispel – help explain why many Serbs in Croatia reject Croatian rule.'[8]

MULTI-PARTY ELECTIONS

In January 1990 the Yugoslav Communist League's Extraordinary 14th Congress was held in Belgrade, and the divergent paths of the different republican leaderships were apparent. The Slovenes pursued the position of making the League an alliance of republican communist parties, whereas the Serbs insisted on the retention of the principle of democratic centralism – although there were already strong confederal elements in the League. There was a failure to reach agreement, the Slovene delegation walked out, and the Congress was adjourned until a consensus position could be agreed. On 22 January the leading role of the Communist League was removed from the constitution, and at its reconvened meeting in May 1990 the Congress dissolved the League, thus ending Tito's vision of brotherhood and unity under the leadership of the communist movement. Multi-party elections followed soon afterwards – they never took place at a federal level – in all republics, although as Woodward points out: 'The demand for elections did not originate from popular pressure, but with politicians seeking more political power over their territories and opposition intellectuals seeking more political influence over the course of events.'[9] Markovic had intended that federal elections would be held towards the end of the year, after the republican elections had been completed. However, this step, which would have allowed the views of Yugoslavs as a whole to be expressed, was vetoed by Slovenia, as was a referendum on the future of the country, planned for 1990.

Overall, the communists had varying degrees of success in the elections. In April 1990, in Slovenia, where they had played a leading role in the democratic transition, transforming themselves into what was basically a social democratic party – the Party of Democratic Renewal – and arguing for confederal status within Yugoslavia, or independence outside, they emerged as the largest single party. They also won the presidency, with Milan Kucan elected on 59 per cent of the vote, but the right to form the government went to DEMOS, a six-party, centre-right coalition led by the Christian Democrats. All parties, however, favoured the maximum sovereignty for Slovenia.

In Croatia elections were held in April and May 1990, where the communists, renamed the Croatian League of Communists/Party of Democratic Change, were defeated – with 25 per cent of the vote – by the Croatian Democratic Union (HDZ) – with 42 per cent of the vote, translating into over two-thirds of parliamentary seats. The HDZ campaigned 'on a platform stressing family, prosperity, God, and the Croatian nation'.[10] Franjo Tudjman of the HDZ was elected as president, in an anti-semitic, anti-Serb campaign under slogans such as 'a thousand years of uninterrupted Croatian statehood'.[11] Indeed, as Crnobrnja points out: 'Tudjman and HDZ lost no time in consolidating their victory in the most provocative way possible: by making sure that Croatia would constitutionally become a state of Croats.'[12] They ignored the 600,000 Serbs in Croatia who were deprived of their status as a constituent nation of the republic and lost their minority rights. This created an ethnic basis for the Croatian state, which raised extremely disturbing images from the Second World War Independent State of Croatia, especially as Tudjman asserted that it had been a legitimate expression of Croat statehood. Slogans like 'Croatia for the Croats only', led to excesses against the Serbs, who were not only pushed out of their positions in the police force – a move authorized by the Croatian government, but also from posts in administration and enterprises. According to Lampe, 'local Croats also sacked or seized Serbian-owned vacation houses along the Adriatic coast'.[13]

In Serbia multi-party elections took place in December 1990, and the Socialist Party of Serbia (SPS) – formed from a merger of the Serbian Communist League and the mass organization, the Socialist Alliance of Working People of Serbia – under the leadership of Slobodan Milosevic, won 65 per cent of votes cast, securing 77 per cent of parliamentary seats. The largest opposition party was the anti-communist, nationalist Serbian Movement for Renewal, led by Vuk Draskovic, which won 16 per cent of the vote, gaining 19 seats in parliament. Milosevic was also elected as President with two-thirds of the vote. The Albanians in Kosovo boycotted the elections to indicate their opposition to Belgrade's policies, but this had the effect of allowing the SPS to predominate in Kosovo. (The Albanian delegates in the Kosovo assembly had already, on 2 July, declared political sovereignty for Kosovo, effectively opting for republican status within the federal system. In response, the Serbian government had dissolved the Kosovan assembly and begun a purge of Albanians in government and media.) The Serbian communist leadership had initially opposed the introduction of multi-party democracy, and did not favour the system change that was being pursued in other republics within Yugoslavia. Likewise in Montenegro, the communists had not favoured system change, nor did they change the name of their party, and they maintained their commitment to communist politics including self-management, winning in the process widespread popular support and achieving over 66 per cent of seats in the multi-party elections in December 1990.

In Macedonia, multi-party elections took place in November and December 1990, with the communists, also maintaining their name – with the suffix Party of Democratic Change – and pro-Yugoslav position, performing well in the first round, but losing out to the revived historic party, the Internal Macedonian Revolutionary Organization (IMRO) in the second. The result was 37 seats for IMRO and 31 for the communists, leading to a multi-party coalition government led by the communist Gligorov. In Bosnia-Hercegovina, where the population was clearly divided into different national groups, voters primarily voted on national lines, with the communists achieving only 6 per cent of the vote, the Serbian Democratic Party (SDS), led by Radovan Karadzic 29.6 per cent, the Croatian Democratic Union (HDZ) 18.3 per cent and the predominantly Muslim Party of Democratic Action (SDA) 33.8 per cent. A coalition government was formed of all three national parties, led by Alija Izetbegovic, leader of the SDA, on the basis of a trilateral power-sharing agreement modelled on the structures of the federal government.

There was no Yugoslav-wide party operating during all these elections, although there were attempts made to reforge the League of Communists-Movement for Yugoslavia, based in the Yugoslav army, the JNA, later that year. As Seroka points out: 'The Yugoslav national army was the backbone of support for a united Yugoslav League of Communists. Its mission was to defend the party, and virtually all its officers were party members.'[14] In fact, its mission was to defend a united socialist Yugoslavia, and with the disbanding of the Communist League, its leaders founded the League of Communists-Movement for Yugoslavia with a membership across the federation of 250,000, and in the subsequent period, the JNA sought – if rather ineffectually – to maintain the integrity of Yugoslavia.

The election results showed, therefore, either a considerable or reasonable level of support for communist or former communist parties in most republics – for the relatively unreformed parties in Montenegro, Macedonia and Serbia, and for those transformed into social democratic parties in Croatia and Slovenia. Only in Bosnia-Hercegovina were the communists resoundingly defeated with voters supporting nationally based parties.

Slovenia was a fairly straightforward case of a desire for western integration on the basis of politics somewhat like that of the German Social Democratic Party which was provided by the transformed communists – as was the case subsequently with the former communist Hungarian Socialist Party, and the Social Democracy of the Republic of Poland, both of which joined the Socialist International, introduced neo-liberal economic reform programmes when they came to power in their countries in 1994 and 1993 respectively, and pursued membership of the EU and NATO. In Croatia, petit-bourgeois national aspirations made the HDZ the largest single party; nevertheless, there was still a considerable base of support for the communists, reflecting the political divisions that had arisen there during the development of strong pro-market forces from the 1970s onwards. In Macedonia, there was relatively little demand for system change, although the revival of IMRO indicated concerns for the future of Macedonia in a fragmenting Yugoslavia. Serbia and Montenegro remained committed to the maintenance of the Yugoslav federation and opposition – with considerable popular support – to the opening up to full marketization and neo-liberal economic policies.

The drive towards republican independence and secession was clearly a strong factor in these elections, but it is notable that 'no party claiming an independent state had a majority; all formed coalition governments'.[15] Indeed, the issue of nationalism was a complex one also, because it was a factor at two different levels. There was, as Woodward points out, the issue of the national self-determination of the republics in relation to the federal government. Then there was also the issue of the 'political rights of constituent nations to self-determination regardless of their members' republic of residence'.[16] This was clearly of great significance in the case of the Serbs of Croatia and the Serbs, Croats and Muslims in Bosnia-Hercegovina. A disturbing feature of the elections was that constitutional restrictions on free speech, designed to protect minorities and prevent 'incitement of national, racial or religious hatred', were ignored, and minorities became fair

game to electoral expediency, whether they were Albanians in
Kosovo or Macedonia, or Serbs or Jews in Croatia.[17]

The multi-party elections and party modifications were, of course,
taking place against the background of system change in central and
eastern Europe as a whole, since 1989. With the fall of the Berlin
Wall in November 1989 and the introduction of multi-party systems
to the region, all former ruling communist parties underwent some
form of political and structural transformation – to a greater or
lesser extent. Making a comparison with the electoral performance
of communist or former communist parties in other former socialist
countries, it can be seen that, with the exception of Bosnia-Hercegovina, the communist or former communist parties in Yugoslavia
performed vastly better in the first free elections than did their
counterparts in central Europe. In Hungary and Poland it seemed
as if the former communists had been wiped from the political
map in the first free elections – they did of course return to power
with mass popular support in the second elections as the economic
consequences of neo-liberal economic reform began to hit the
voters. The levels of electoral support for communist or former
communist parties in many of the Yugoslav republics more closely
paralleled the popular backing for such parties in Bulgaria and
Romania, where in the first post-1989 multi-party elections, the
former communist parties were returned to power with considerable popular support.

BREAKDOWN

With the demise of the League, discussions about the future of
Yugoslavia moved to the federal parliament. The Serbs, supported
by the Montenegrins, argued for a federation, not least because so
many Serbs lived outside Serbia. The Croats and Slovenes favoured
a confederation in which they would have full national sovereignty.
Macedonia and Bosnia-Hercegovina tended towards federation, the
former because it feared the irredentism of Bulgaria, Albania and
Greece and preferred the protection afforded by the Yugoslav state,
and the latter because any break-up of Yugoslavia on national lines
would leave the multi-national Bosnia-Hercegovina in a disastrous
situation. Clearly, it remained the case – as it had been on the
founding of the south slav state – that only a united, multi-national
Yugoslav state could protect, and guarantee the rights of, the diverse

population. The negotiation of some kind of compromise proved unsuccessful, however. The federal government of Ante Markovic was, therefore, faced with some very difficult problems. Markovic, who was a Yugoslav-oriented Croat, favoured the maintenance of a federal state with the introduction of multi-party democracy and free-market economics, which was essentially the position of the IMF, the US and Britain. They wished for Yugoslavia to undergo the same political and economic transition that was taking place elsewhere in central and eastern Europe and for her to remain united. According to Crnobrnja, Markovic was widely perceived to be the main beneficiary of the dissolution of the Yugoslav Communist League, with 'his Cabinet as the only policy-forming body in the federation'.[18] At the same time as his free-market reforms, Markovic pursued a strategy of integration into the institutions of western Europe, seeking associate membership of the European Community, and membership of the Council of Europe. All republican leaders favoured closer links with the Community, and there were great hopes that various types of economic and practical assistance would be made available from the EC and also from the US, which was vocal in its support of Markovic. Indeed, Warren Zimmerman described Markovic as 'a dynamic Croatian committed to economic reform and other western policies', and 'a symbol of everything his country needed'.[19] However, little support was forthcoming, which considerably undermined his position and therefore the possibility of maintaining the federation under the conditions of political and economic transition.

Markovic's position was criticized from two perspectives. The Serbian leadership strongly shared his positions in support of the federation, and also went along with liberalization and economic and political reform – the latter less enthusiastically – but their main criticisms were about the scale and pace of the economic reforms, which they claimed were detrimental to the Serbian economy. Indeed, Markovic's reforms were having a devastating impact on the economy, as outlined in the previous chapter. The Croatian and Slovenian leaderships, on the other hand, strongly criticized Markovic's centralization, which they considered to favour Serbia. In the summer of 1990 Markovic formed his own Yugoslav Reform Party, but the Slovene and Croatian elections had already taken place and it received little support in Serbia and Montenegro. However, it did do fairly well in Macedonia and moderately well in Bosnia-Hercegovina – both republics that had much to gain from the maintenance of the federal state. Markovic had really founded the party to contest in the federal elections, but of course these never took place.

A number of incremental but rapid steps were now taken by both Slovenia and Croatia towards secession, and both declared their sovereignty within Yugoslavia in July 1990, proposing that Yugoslavia should become a confederation of sovereign states. However, whilst there was fairly uniform support for this course in Slovenia, this was not the case in Croatia. The accession to power of the HDZ government in Croatia, with its strongly nationalist platform – which included the reintroduction of the symbols of the Ustasa state – led to anxiety and protest on the part of the Serbian community in Croatia, of considerable size in the Krajina. In August 1990 the towns of Knin and Benkovac blockaded themselves against the Croatian police, organizing a defence militia to resist Croatization. During the summer of 1990, Tudjman began to organize paramilitary units, which put him in conflict with the JNA, but he took this step because he knew 'that the federal army would never participate in the Croatization of the Serbian parts of Croatia'.[20] In October 1990 an Autonomous Region of Krajina was declared around Knin – where there had been strong electoral support for the former communist party – as the Croatian government was clearly moving towards the declaration of an independent Croatia, founded on an ethnic Croatian identity. In December 1990 the Croatian parliament adopted the republic's new constitution, asserting Croatia's sovereignty and its right to secede.

Following the election of the governments of Slovenia and Croatia in spring 1990, the JNA ordered that the arms of the territorial defence forces should be handed over to the JNA. Most of the Croatian weaponry was secured, but Slovenia retained large quantities of weapons, which it used to arm the nascent illegal Slovenian army, supplemented by illegal arms imports through Hungary. The Croats took rapid steps to arm themselves, mostly funded by Croatian nationalist émigrés. In January 1991 the federal presidency appeared to make finally a real attempt to halt the imminent disintegration of the federation. It gave the Slovene and Croatian territorial defence forces a 10-day deadline to give up their weapons. On 23 January the JNA was placed on alert to enforce the deadline, but two days later the federal presidency withdrew the order. The JNA strongly supported going ahead with the order, but the federal presidency decided to back off from a military confrontation with the two republics. This was, according to East and Pontin, despite 'televised evidence of Croatia's arms procurement programme'.[21] The formal announcement of the founding of a Croatian regular army was made on 28 May 1991.

This was the moment when the federal government could have made a constitutional stand, backed by the JNA, to prevent unilateral secession from the federation, and the infringement of the international recognition of Yugoslavia's boundaries. The federal presidency, however, had by this time become enormously weakened and was probably unable by this point to fight for the integrity of Yugoslavia.

From autumn 1990, realizing that Markovic was unable to bring forth western aid to ameliorate the terrible results of his economic reforms, the republics had abandoned the economic reform programme. 'Government expenditures rose in all republics; the process of privatisation was stopped, cancelled, or delayed, with social property being nationalized equally vigorously in "socialist" Serbia and the "Western-oriented and capitalist" Croatia and Slovenia.'[22] The federal government had lost all control over the reform programme and clearly the republican governments no longer felt that they had to abide by federal agreements. Thus, when Slovenia actually seceded in June 1991, despite an attempt by the JNA to prevent it, the horse had in effect already bolted. While the federal government might have had the political inclination to hold the federation together, it did not have the political strength.

The Croatian parliament's assertion of the right to secede, was followed in February by the declaration of the Autonomous Region of Krajina of secession from Croatia. In May the Autonomous Region held a referendum which opted to remain part of Yugoslavia, and a week later a Croatian referendum voted by 90 per cent in favour of secession from Yugoslavia. The first violence in Croatia took place in the town of Pakrac in western Slavonia, when the Ministry of the Interior attempted to change the predominantly Serb personnel of the local police force. The Serb population protested, violence broke out, and the JNA intervened. Subsequently, a confrontation took place in Plitvice national park, and barricades were constructed all around Vukovar. In May 1991 the Croatian militia attacked the Serb village of Borovo Selo where they met fierce opposition, leading to the deaths of 17 militia and 20 civilians. Following that, there were regular skirmishes and killings until full-scale war finally broke out. During this period, Milosevic and Tudjman met secretly, both alone and, on occasions, with Izetbegovic, but a peaceful resolution to the conflict was not forthcoming. In May 1991 Jacques Delors, at that time president of the EC Commission, and Jacques Santer of Luxembourg, visited Yugoslavia, promising aid if there was a peaceful settlement. US Secretary of State, James Baker, also visited, urging support for Markovic's government and the economic reforms, and opposing the secession of Slovenia and Croatia.

However, both the EC and US had already made statements that in effect bolstered Slovenian and Croatian ambitions. In January 1991 US Ambassador Zimmerman had publicly warned that the US would not accept 'the use of force to hold Yugoslavia together', and that 'it would consider illegitimate the army's definition of its constitutional obligation to defend the borders of the state from internal threats'.[23] On 13 March 1991 the European Parliament had resolved, 'that the constituent republics and autonomous provinces of Yugoslavia must have the right freely to determine their own future in a peaceful and democratic manner and on the basis of recognized international and national borders'.[24]

On 25 June 1991 Slovenia unilaterally proclaimed its independence, followed the next day by Croatia. Under international law, this step was, in fact, illegal, because the international frontiers of Yugoslavia were recognized under the Final Act at Helsinki in 1975. Changes to these frontiers could not be made without 'the consent of the governments and peoples concerned. In Yugoslavia's case, neither the federal government of Yugoslavia nor the peoples living in Yugoslavia were ever comprehensively consulted.'[25]

SLOVENIAN SECESSION

Hostilities began on 27 June 1991 as Markovic signed the order for the JNA to begin action in Slovenia. The JNA's plan was to secure Slovenia's international borders with the 2,000 JNA troops stationed in the republic. These were primarily conscripts doing their national service and were lightly armed. The Slovenes, on the other hand, had been preparing their forces for this purpose, and mobilized 21,000 troops. According to Lampe, 'the purchase of new anti-tank and anti-aircraft ordinance and the assembling of an intelligence network within the JNA set the rest of the stage for a stunning success'.[26] As the JNA moved their troops to the border posts, they found themselves cut off by road blocks and surrounded. A fall-back plan of JNA occupation of Slovenia, backed up by air bombardment, was not pursued, and a cease-fire was negotiated by the troika of EC foreign ministers on 4 July, the death toll being 67. Croatia and Slovenia were persuaded by the troika to postpone their declarations of independence for three months as a face-saving device. On 18 July the federal leadership agreed to the withdrawal of the JNA – for a supposedly temporary period – within three months; in effect Yugoslav withdrawal was really a de facto recognition of Slovene independence.

As the JNA was the defender of the federal Yugoslavia, it was the cause of considerable surprise that it did not make more vigorous attempts to prevent Slovenia leaving the federation, or play a more direct role in opposing the secessionist forces, which had begun to appeal to NATO 'to intervene on their behalf'.[27] According to Norah Beloff, however, the JNA leadership were fully aware of the dynamics of the situation and the likely tragic outcome of the break-up of the state and they did come close to attempting a more direct role. Veljko Kadijevic, head of the JNA, favoured military action, and advised Borislav Jovic, chair of the federal presidency, in February 1991, that

> the JNA must take preventative action against what he saw as a German plot to break up the Yugoslav state, which he was sure would lead to civil war. Kadijevic gave Jovic a written draft which would have authorised the army to treat advocates of secession as traitors. During that month, the Yugoslav intelligence services infiltrated the Croat secessionists and were able to show pictures of the Croat minister of defence, Martin Spegelj, discussing plans to send Croat units to surround and where necessary, to slaughter JNA officers and their families.[28]

Spegelj's arrest was ordered by the federal military prosecutor, but he was instead hidden by the Croatian government.

Kadijevic also visited Moscow in March 1991 to seek Soviet support for the JNA if it mobilized against the secessionists, but help was not forthcoming. Following this, Kadijevic asserted that he was going to go ahead and arrest secessionist leaders, with or without the backing of the federal leadership, and even take control of the government, but he did not ultimately do this. Benson suggests that: 'Kadijevic in the end gambled on the restoration of hard-line authority in the USSR as the source of salvation.'[29] After the failure of the attempts to this end in the Soviet Union in the summer of 1991, however, this was no longer a possibility.

Thus, the re-Balkanization of the south slav lands began when Slovenia – and Croatia – were recognized as independent states by Germany in December 1991, and by the EC in January 1992, following the report of the Badinter Commission. However, the first phase of war in Croatia was to unfold before that took place.

6
War: the first wave – Croatia

The secession of Slovenia from the federal republic was relatively bloodless, but this was not to be the case with Croatia – thousands died in the process. For this foreign governments must bear considerable responsibility, by encouraging both Slovenian and Croatian secessionism, in a context in which the risk of widespread conflict was increasing. Without the prospect – and eventual achievement – of international recognition, and the acceptance by a number of foreign states of the arguments of the nationalists, it is possible that a negotiated settlement could have been arrived at which would either have maintained some form of Yugoslavia, or achieved a peaceful dissolution. The foreign backing of separatists made war inevitable and, as Adam Burgess observes: 'Without the international encouragement of Croatian and Bosnian Muslim nationalism, deals could have been struck at any number of points.'[1] The German government of the time was particularly irresponsible: former US Secretary of State and UN envoy Cyrus Vance, referring to German Foreign Minister Hans-Dietrich Genscher, described the war as 'Mr Genscher's war' because of Germany's push to recognize separatists in Slovenia and Croatia.[2] Indeed, as Misha Glenny observes: 'By the autumn of 1991, Hans-Dietrich Genscher had made the recognition of Slovenia and Croatia his own personal crusade.'[3] However, other states such as the US and European powers that in theory supported Yugoslav integrity, rendered this support meaningless by stating – as Douglas Hurd did, for example, after the JNA responded to the Slovenian secession – that 'this should not include the use of force'.[4]

The catalyst for the first wave of bloody war in Yugoslavia was the new constitution introduced by the ultra-nationalist government of Franjo Tudjman in Croatia, which stripped the Serbs in Croatia of many of their rights, refusing, amongst other things, to accept the right of the Serbian minority within Croatia – a majority in the Krajina – to self-determination. The Yugoslav constitution provided that:

> The nations of Yugoslavia, proceeding from the right of every nation to self-determination, including the right to secession ... have ... united in a federal republic of free and equal nations and nationalities and founded a socialist federal community.[5]

This reference to the 'nations', did not mean the territorially-defined republics but the six national constituent peoples of Yugoslavia – as explained in Chapter 4. Clearly this did not present a problem in Slovenia, for as Judah observes:

> As Slovenia had no native-born minorities and there were no pockets of Slovenes outside the republic, the issue was clear-cut: republic and nation were the same thing. By contrast, Milosevic argued that the Croats had a right to self-determination, but that they could not take Serbs out of Yugoslavia against their will.[6]

Clearly the Serbian minority in Croatia did not, on the whole, wish to be taken out of Yugoslavia. The Serbian community in Croatia had suffered mass slaughter at the hands of Croatian fascists during the Second World War and did not wish to be ruled by the HDZ government in Zagreb, which stripped the Serbs of their constitutional protections and rehabilitated the Ustasa regime. Serbs were driven out of a range of professions, and Serbian homes were dynamited in cities like Zagreb and Dubrovnik. Thus, a vote in the Serb-inhabited areas in May 1991 supported secession from Croatia, declaring themselves an autonomous region, and opting to remain within Yugoslavia – which they had the right to do under the Yugoslav constitution. The JNA, which had withdrawn from Slovenia, now, in the summer of 1991, moved first to act as a buffer between the new Croatian National Guard and the Serbian defence forces and eventually effectively to support the Croatian Serbs, until the cease-fire between Croatia and the Yugoslav authorities in January 1992. The Krajina became a demili-tarized zone patrolled by 10,000 UN peacekeepers and, in April 1992, the Croatian Serbs' National Council established the Republic of Serbian Krajina, comprising 30 per cent of Croatian territory. In August 1995 overwhelming forces – rearmed and trained by the US and Germany – invaded Serbian Krajina and occupied the territory. Some 300,000 Croatian-Serb refugees fled to Yugoslavia in the largest ethnic cleansing of the whole period of the break-up of Yugoslavia. This Croatian victory was used – in combination with massive NATO bombing of Bosnian Serb targets – to pressurize the Bosnian Serbs into accepting the peace negotiations that ended in the Dayton Accords.

INTERNATIONAL INTERESTS

International backing for independence emerged from Austria, Denmark, Hungary and Switzerland, but clearly German support would be decisive for Croatia at a time when Britain, France, the US and Russia all still basically supported a united Yugoslavia. Woodward observes that Tudjman's government had frequent consultations in Bonn about a strategy for independence, and that the Vatican, which strongly lobbied in support of Croatian and Slovenian independence, had considerable influence on the Bavarian CSU and through that the CDU. In addition: 'Jorg Reismuller, publisher of the *Frankfurter Allgemeine Zeitung*, the most influential German newspaper, was particularly sympathetic to the Croatian prospect of independence and waged a campaign against Slobodan Milosevic and Serbian nationalism that had a major role in shaping German opinion about the conflict.'[7]

However, Germany has also been credited with having a longer involvement in the push for an independent Croatia. According to some commentators, the German intelligence agency, the BND, had been involved in the training of Croatian separatists, led by remnants of the Ustasa since the 1960s. German intelligence analyst Eric Schmidt-Eenboom has observed:

In the early 60s, the BND decided to cooperate fully with the Ustasa. This became plain to see after the Croat Spring in the beginning of the 1970s. After Tito's death they accelerated their efforts together with the Ustasa in order to disintegrate Yugoslavia into several smaller states.[8]

This view has been confirmed by the Croatian Antun Duhacek, former Director of Yugoslav Counter Intelligence: 'The Germans wanted an absolute and complete subordination of Croatian intelligence that would carry out all that the Germans wanted, and the Germans promised that this would be in the interests of the future independent, free Croatia.'[9] Such activities continued during the 1980s, according to Sean Gervasi, from the Institute for European Studies:

> The German Secret Service was enormously active in Croatia and in all of Yugoslavia trying in the 1980s to build bridges between what were called the national communists – Stipe Mesic, Franjo Tudjman in Yugoslavia – and the Ustasa revanchist organisations which live in the Diaspora of Croatia, that is to say, all of the people of weight and influence who had fled the former Nazi puppet state in 1945.[10]

Covert German support for Croatian independence also continued during the military conflict with the JNA. David C. Hackworth, military correspondent for *Newsweek* reported that the German government had broken the international arms embargo and that he had himself observed arms deliveries at Split and Croatian ports along the Dalmatian coast. Gregory Copley, editor of *Strategic Policy*, confirmed that a Croatian MiG-21, shot down over the Krajina – reported by the Croats to be former JNA stock – was actually thinly disguised former East German stock, channelled to Croatia by the German government. In his view it would have been impossible for such heavy equipment to have been supplied by anything other than a government.[11] Not surprisingly, this type of activity was enormously resented by those who wished to maintain a unified Yugoslavia. As Misha Glenny observes, referring to German and Austrian enthusiasm for the recognition of Slovenia and Croatia: 'The German and Austrian positions reflected both countries' economic, cultural and historical interests in the region, but in Serbia they were perceived to represent the imperialist expansion of a unified German state into Eastern Europe.'[12]

CONFLICT WITH THE JNA

The possibility of a negotiated solution to the crisis received a terminal blow in the summer of 1991, as President Tudjman of Croatia first boycotted meetings of the federal presidency in July, and then on 4 August broke off all relations with Serbia.[13] Soon thereafter, the armed confrontations that had been blowing up between Croatian Serbs and Croatian government forces were to become primarily a war between the Croatian government and the JNA. The JNA had a federal responsibility impartially to maintain civil order, but this was no longer accepted by the Croatian government. Defence minister Spegelj wanted to drive the JNA from their barracks in Croatia and to seize their weapons, although Tudjman held back from this, while building up the Croatian National Guard as an independent army. The opposition of the JNA to secessionism, in support of the Yugoslav constitution, meant that in Slovenia and Croatia it was often perceived to be pro-Serb. Indeed, there was also some residual hostility towards the JNA in Croatia because of its role in reining in the nationalist movement there in the early 1970s.

> In 1970–71 repeated army warnings to Tito about the danger of the mass nationalist movement developing in Croatia and of its links to groups in foreign countries (especially guest workers and émigrés in Germany) led the president and the highest party circles finally to act in December 1971, and bring the movement to a halt through party discipline on Croatian leaders.[14]

However, the real issue was that, while the JNA had a responsibility to protect Serbs who had a constitutional right to remain in Yugoslavia, from the point of view of the Croatian government this was an infringement of their sovereignty, and they saw the Serbian defence forces and authorities in the Krajina as rebels whom it was legitimate to defeat militarily. In fact, Croatia was not legitimately a sovereign state, and under international law the boundaries and constitution of Yugoslavia were still applicable. The first direct conflict between the JNA and the Croatian National Guard took place near the town of Vukovar. The town itself had a Croat majority, but the local region (*opstina*) had a Serb majority, and when the government replaced the locally-elected assembly with a governor appointed in Zagreb, it was rejected by the Serbs in the Vukovar *opstina*. The Croats then attempted to enforce this with their militia and this became a turning point in events in Croatia, because the JNA, until this point having been enforcers of civil order, 'for the first time sided openly with the Serb "freedom fighters"'.[15] The Croats, according to Crnobrnja, 'jumped on this opportunity and started an all out anti-JNA campaign'.[16] Tudjman insisted that the JNA give up its civil order function and go back to barracks, and in August 1991 ordered a general mobilization in Croatia to fight for independence. The response of the JNA was that it was constitutionally obliged to protect the integrity of

Yugoslavia and was answerable to the federal presidency and not Tudjman. JNA units were also authorized to return fire if attacked.

Crnobrnja argues that Tudjman was not confident that the Croatian army could defeat the JNA, together with Serbian local defence forces in Croatia – which were based on the Territorial Defence reservist forces, previously linked to the Communist League – and volunteers who were now coming from Serbia. In their favour the Croats had the benefit of a number of Croat JNA commanders who transferred themselves and their weaponry to the Croat side, and also illegal arms imports – in contravention of the EC and UN arms embargoes that were now in place. The Croats also hoped to benefit from the perceived weakness of the JNA – that it did not apply full force to the constitutional aim of preserving the territorial integrity of Yugoslavia. However, according to Crnobrnja, the Croatian 'strategic aim was not a military but a political and diplomatic victory', where a temporary loss of territory would be made up for by international recognition of Croatian independence. This would be enhanced by provoking the JNA into 'the type of action that would lead to international condemnation, thus securing sympathy and support for the Croatian cause. Germany was already preparing to orchestrate full media support for Croatia if the JNA were drawn deeper into the conflict.'[17] The JNA was in an increasingly difficult situation, for not only did the Croatian government decide to blockade the JNA barracks and cut off their supplies, but they were also beginning to face the withdrawal of further funding and recruits from many of the republics – with the exception of Serbia and Montenegro. What had been a genuinely multi-national Yugoslav army was now becoming increasingly dependent on Serbia and Montenegro, as the Croats continued the false argument first put forward by the Slovenians – that the JNA was an army of occupation. The JNA was the army of Slovenia and Croatia as much as it was the army of any other republic in Yugoslavia – what had changed was that Slovenia and Croatia had illegally and unilaterally declared independence and built their own armies because they knew they could not rely on the JNA to further their own secessionist interests. Because, therefore, of the pan-Yugoslav position of the JNA, the secessionists formed their own paramilitary organizations, and the Croatian Serbs activated their territorial defence reservist forces.

According to Crnobrnja:

> The Serbs in Croatia, after being subjected to a systematic campaign of Croatomania, in which they lost the right to use their alphabet, lost jobs, were harassed by Croatian ultra-nationalists, saw their houses blown up, and so on, organized strong militia and paramilitary forces that took an active part in the war in Croatia.[18]

At the same time volunteers were arriving from Serbia to fight alongside the Croatian Serbs, and these were often ultra-nationalist, highly-motivated individuals, who frequently took up the traditional symbols of the Chetnik movement. On the Croatian side Ustasa units were formed, taking up the symbols of the fascist period, and they were joined by a number of volunteers from far-right groups in other parts of Europe. Feelings ran extremely high, and in Serbia there was intense outrage about the treatment of Serbs in Croatia. Vuk Draskovic, who was Serbia's leading political opposition figure, stated in the summer of 1991: 'The Serbian state must take it upon itself to defend the Serbian people in those parts of Croatia where they constitute a majority ... Serbia must punish those who threaten Serbs, demolish their homes, and force them to migrate.'[19]

With the recognition by the JNA leadership that the secession of Slovenia was the definitive end of Yugoslavia as it had been, their approach to their role did begin to change. As noted above, with the conflict in Vukovar, for the first time the JNA actively confronted the Croatian forces, fighting in defence of Serbian rights, rather than merely seeking to act as a buffer between the opposing sides. As JNA leader Kadijevic pointed out, from the point of the secession of Slovenia and the end of the old Yugoslavia,

> we moved to the second concept of creating the new Yugoslavia. When the Croats started to attack the Serbian people in Croatia we co-operated with the TO in those areas and gave the people weapons and so on ... as for the borders there was a clear idea, that is that they should be where there was a majority of Serbian people. If Croatia wanted to go that was okay but they could not take the Serbs with them.[20]

The conflict in Croatia was a war on two fronts: on the one hand, the struggle for control by the JNA and Serb forces of Serb-occupied territories, which constituted between a third and a quarter of Croatia – around Knin, in central Croatia, and in eastern Slavonia; on the other hand, from 14 September, the siege of JNA barracks by Croatian forces in the rest of Croatia. As Silber and Little observe:

> Behind Serb lines the JNA was free to group and regroup as the demands of battle required. Behind Croat lines it was immobilized. In almost every important town in the republic, the JNA was trapped in its barracks, its guns trained outward, surrounded by the Croatian National Guard, guns trained inward, in an explosive stand-off.[21]

The fate of the besieged JNA garrisons varied. In Gospic, for example, a battle broke out which ended with the defeat of the JNA and the killing of the JNA commander. In other places, the JNA withdrew, sometimes in military order with its weaponry intact, and at Varazdin the JNA surrendered, leaving its equipment behind.

When the besieging of JNA barracks began on 14 September 1991, the conflict intensified. The JNA responded in territories where it was mobile, by backing up local Serb units with heavy fire-power to consolidate Serb control. In Vukovar and its suburbs, for example, where sporadic fighting and bombardment had been taking place since July 1991, a full-scale siege to gain control of the city was commenced, eventually ending with the fall of Vukovar on 20 November.

Another key centre of conflict was the port city of Dubrovnik. On 25 August 1991 Croatian forces attacked a JNA base in the Bay of Kotor along the coast from Dubrovnik. The Croatian forces were repulsed by the JNA with heavy losses, and JNA forces from Montenegro then fought their way up the coast, confronting Croatian forces near Dubrovnik, imposing a naval blockade and laying siege to the city. Contrary to media reports at that time, which asserted that the old town of Dubrovnik had been virtually destroyed, it was, according to Mark Almond, left relatively unscathed.[22] Nevertheless, pro-Croatian media in western countries were able successfully to give the impression that 'the Serbs' were the aggressors and had destroyed this beautiful ancient city – 'the pearl of the Adriatic'. During this period, in fact, the Croatian government was being advised by a Washington-based PR firm, which was doing much to create Croatia's international image as the victim of the Serbs.[23] As Adam Burgess has commented:

The Croatian leadership dramatised, and to an extent even provoked, the attacks on the cities of Vukovar and Dubrovnik by the Yugoslav army. The international, particularly German, response was to accept that these confrontations, and increasingly that the overall situation, was simply one of Serb aggression and Croatian victimhood. This emboldened the Croats to go further. Through Vukovar and Dubrovnik, the Croats confirmed for themselves that propaganda and presentation to the 'international community' were their key resources.[24]

The primary target of the JNA bombardment was the city's suburbs, where the tourist hotels were located: many of these had been turned into barracks by Croatian forces. After November the conflict settled, as Silber and Little observe, into a low-level stand-off.[25] In May 1992, some months after the cease-fire was agreed in Croatia, a truce was finalized in Dubrovnik.

Following the fall of Vukovar, the JNA and Serb units moved to consolidate their control of eastern Slavonia, which secured the aims of the federal forces – to establish the viability and cohesion of the Serbian territories in Croatia. Simultaneously, 'President Tudjman, under international pressure, agreed to the de-blocking of the JNA's Marshal Tito barracks in Zagreb.'[26] This earned him the hostility of the more extreme elements amongst the Croat leadership who felt that he was giving up too much in order to gain international respectability and that the Croatian defeat of Vukovar should be avenged or reversed. Clearly, Tudjman was in favour of consolidating his position and did not favour a protracted war with the JNA at this point. According to Judah: 'Tudjman feared that if he did not stop the war he would lose more territory. It was better to halt the war until such time as his army was ready to retake the lost territories.'[27]

In fact, the federal presidency – which now consisted only of Serbia and Montenegro, as Croatia and Slovenia had withdrawn and Macedonia and Bosnia-Hercegovina stopped attending during the Croatian war – had also decided to conclude the war at this point, although it is possible that they could have pressed for further victories. According to Panic, JNA commander in Croatia, after victories in eastern Slavonia following the fall of Vukovar, they could have been in Zagreb in two days, but this was opposed by Milosevic:

The moment Vukovar fell, Croatia lost the war. Because we could have marched to Zagreb without any problems ... But then I was ordered to go back. I talked to Jovic, and Kostic. And I also talked to President Milosevic. It was his decision, Milosevic's decision and it was approved by the rump presidency. He simply said, 'We have no job there in Croat populated areas. We have to protect the Serb areas,' and that was the line.[28]

UN mediator Cyrus Vance worked in the latter part of 1991 to arrive at a lasting cease-fire agreement, which was eventually achieved, including the deployment of 10,000 UN international peace-keeping troops in Croatia, who would act as a buffer between the Croats and Serbs, patrolling the Serb-occupied areas as a demilitarized zone. This agreement, as Mark Almond describes it, 'favoured the status quo brought about since June',[29] and on 2 January 1992, after 14 failed cease-fires over the previous few months, a final cease-fire was signed at Sarajevo by the military representatives of Croatia and Yugoslavia.

NEGOTIATION AND RECOGNITION

Although it was UN mediator Cyrus Vance who ultimately brought about the agreement, the European Community had made a number of unsuccessful efforts to negotiate a cease-fire. They had, however, clearly moved away from the position of supporting the integrity of Yugoslavia before the hostilities in Croatia broke out. The initial position of the EC, which had been adopted in November 1989 when Yugoslavia applied for associate member status of the EC, was 'to uphold the unity of and democratic transformations in Yugoslavia'.[30] This position lasted until the declarations of independence by Slovenia and Croatia. By the end of the conflict in Slovenia, the EC had changed its position, as was apparent from a statement in July from the EC's Foreign Affairs Council, which chose to stress, 'that "it is on the people of Yugoslavia to decide their future," to express "firm opposition to the use of force," and to "note that in Yugoslavia all parties concerned accept the reality that a new situation has arisen." For the first time there was no mention of the "unity and integrity of Yugoslavia".'[31] EC negotiators had helped to resolve the conflict with Slovenia through the Brioni Agreement, and had sent in monitors under the Conference on Security and Co-operation in Europe (CSCE) to oversee the terms of the Agreement.

During the summer of 1991, the EC attempted to draw up political principles on the basis of which a solution might be negotiated. The EC concluded that it was unacceptable to bring about changes to internal or international borders through the use of force, that the rights of peoples and minorities in all the republics must be respected in any solution, and that the EC would not accept a policy of fait accompli.[32] One of the key weaknesses of the EC position, however, was that it accepted the nationalist framework for solutions to the crisis, and ignored massive demonstrations that took place – for example, in July 1991, 50,000 marched in Sarajevo in support of a united Yugoslavia, and huge demonstrations for peace took place in Belgrade, Sarajevo and Skopje. However, as Woodward points out:

> The EC had ignored the origins of the conflict – the economic decline, market reforms, and quarrels over the political reform necessary to them – and had accepted the representation of the conflict and possible solutions posed by radical nationalist governments in Slovenia, Croatia and Serbia. It had opened the door to war in Croatia and Bosnia-Hercegovina, and was in the process of depriving the moderates, non-nationalists, southerners, federal government, and majority of the population caught in an ethnically complex situation of any representation or say in the matter.[33]

The above-mentioned principles constituted the basis on which the EC-sponsored Conference on Yugoslavia was convened at the Hague, on 7 September 1991, chaired by the former British foreign secretary, Lord Carrington. The conference aimed to arrive at arrangements for a peaceful accommodation for the Yugoslav peoples, agreeing to take into account all legitimate concerns and aspirations in its attempts to arrive at a peaceful settlement. The Conference was a slow process, and Carrington was criticized for holding short and infrequent plenary sessions and not allowing discussion between the Yugoslav participants. The Conference was also dogged by a lack of focus and direction on the part of the EC, including contradictory positions from EC member states as to whether or not foreign troops should be introduced. Many cease-fires were signed, but did not hold, and an EC embargo on arms sales to Yugoslavia was reinforced by UN Security Council Resolution 713 on 25 September. The effectiveness of these embargoes was, however, highly doubtful. Carrington then tried to establish a framework that would be acceptable to all the republics, including making proposals on varying degrees of independence and free association. Carrington attempted to work his way towards a solution which would allow those republics that wished to maintain a federal state to do so, linked in free association to those who wished for independence.

However, in the context of these Conference negotiations, Germany unilaterally recognized Slovenian and Croatian independence on 23 December 1991, which effectively broke up the Conference and ended any possibility of its achieving a compromise. There was no longer any need for Slovenia and Croatia to participate in discussions about an overall settlement. The Serbs of Krajina, Slavonia and Srem joined together on 24 December, declaring a Serbian republic. This move by Germany to recognition of Croatia was a step that Chancellor Kohl hailed, at his Party Congress that same month, as a victory for German foreign policy.[34] In effect, Germany forced the EC to do the same – which it did in January 1992 – by refusing to support the Maastricht Treaty unless the EC recognized the secessionist states. This was in spite of the fact that Croatia's minority rights provision did not meet the EC's own criteria. 'The search for Germany's motives', according to Crnobrnja, 'should be directed towards their domestic political and strategic foreign policy interests.'[35]

The EC managed the process of recognition by setting up – on a French initiative – the Badinter Commission under former French minister and jurist Robert Badinter, to work out 'a constitutional and human rights test for would-be independent republics seeking EC recognition'.[36] The Commission invited all the Yugoslav republics to apply for recognition, subject to compliance with various requirements. Croatia, Slovenia, Bosnia-Hercegovina and Macedonia all applied for recognition. Slovenia's application was accepted, as was that of Croatia, following German procurement of a letter from Tudjman agreeing constitutionally to guarantee the human rights of the Serbs – although this never took place. Bosnia-Hercegovina's application was withheld, pending a referendum on independence, the proposal of which, according to Crnobrnja, was a serious error: the constitution of Bosnia-Hercegovina required all matters of general importance to be agreed by consensus of the three national groups, whereas a referendum could be won by the agreement of only two of them. Macedonia's application – which was agreeable to the Commission subject to some constitutional modification – was vetoed by Greece. Greece was concerned about potential Macedonian irredentism towards its own Macedonian territories. Serbia and Montenegro agreed to remain within a common state and constituted the new Federal Republic of Yugoslavia. They did not apply for recognition, pointing out that their sovereignty had already been recognized.

The Badinter Commission declared Yugoslavia's formal status to be a state 'in the process of dissolution'. As Benson has observed, the invention of this concept, previously unknown in international law, justified the dismantling of the borders of a sovereign state, while proclaiming the borders of the successor states inviolable. The result of this

> was to deny the legal existence of Yugoslavia, so cutting the ground from under the feet of the Serbs, and to make lines on maps the object of diplomacy. The Titoist constitutions made peoples, not territorial entities, the bearers of sovereignty in Yugoslavia. By conflating the right of peoples to self-determination (the subject of huge controversy in international law) with the right of republics to secede unilaterally, Badinter created a formula for assisting the break-up of the federation.[37]

Either wilfully or through ignorance of the complexities of the situation, and through accepting 'the nationalists' definition of the conflict, [and] undermining or ignoring the forces working against radical nationalists',[38] the EC contributed not only to the break-up of Yugoslavia, but also – through allowing the Germans to cut short the negotiation process and enforce rapid recognition before the constitutional position of the Serbian communities had been resolved – to ensuring that it would take place in violent circumstances. The German leadership attempted to justify their push to rapid recognition on the grounds that this would curtail the violence. Chancellor Kohl argued, according to Woodward, 'that by internationalising the war, granting recognition of the two republics' rights to national self-determination to signal international protection, they would deter further Serbian aggression (in their view, the cause of the war) and thus bring a quick end to the fighting'.[39] This, of course, was completely wrong, since the fighting had ended because neither side at that time wished to pursue it, and Serbian actions were primarily defensive and therefore likely to be exacerbated rather than deterred by the recognition of a state in which they were under attack. Neither the later violent ethnic cleansing of the Serbs from the Krajina by Croatian forces in 1995, nor the terrible war in Bosnia was prevented by recognition. In fact, these were made inevitable by recognition, because this was granted without resolution of the constitutional questions and without full federal negotiations. Indeed, UN negotiator Cyrus Vance himself warned against recognition of separatist states before a political settlement had been achieved, arguing that recognition would take away the diplomatic leverage he had to try to bring the war in Croatia to an end, and that it could possibly result in Bosnia blowing up.[40]

Tragically, Kohl's flawed reasoning, that recognition would deter further warfare, was, according to Woodward, further used by US Secretary of State James Baker in April 1992 to urge the EC towards recognition of Bosnia-Hercegovina, which the Badinter Commission had held back on. This was a mistake with appalling consequences, about which the US administration had been warned. According to former US state department official George Kenney: 'US intelligence agencies were unanimous in saying that if we recognise Bosnia it will blow up.'[41] Arguably, the US were concerned to have an area of influence in the former Yugoslavia, and US championing of Bosnian independence was a means to achieving this. Former Acting US Secretary of State Lawrence Eagleburger has taken the view that it was domestic political considerations – primarily concern about the large US-Croat vote in the 1992 election campaign between Clinton and Bush – that led to the decision to recognize Bosnia without a political settlement between the Muslims, Serbs and Croats. Whatever the reason, it was however the case, as Lord Carrington himself stated, that 'what the international community – the Europeans, the Americans, the UN – did, made it sure there was going to be conflict'.[42]

7
War: the second wave – Bosnia

By the end of 1991, the process of re-Balkanization was well under way – Slovenia and Croatia had been recognized as independent states. The struggle for and against the further break-up of Yugoslavia now shifted to Bosnia-Hercegovina. While responsibility for the first wave of conflict lay with the EC for embarking on the process of recognition at Germany's instigation, responsibility for the second wave lay with the United States. The dangers of the recognition of Bosnia were widely recognized, since it was clear that the Bosnian Serb community was opposed to leaving Yugoslavia and would resist such a development. While the EC drew back from recognition, the United States moved towards 'conceding a primary sphere of influence over Croatia to Germany and taking on Bosnia as its responsibility'.[1] This drive towards recognition on the part of the US catapulted Bosnia into war, when painstaking negotiations which recognized the concerns of the different parties, and the constitutional framework for change, could well have concluded the matter differently. Throughout the war the US systematically blocked peace initiatives by encouraging the Izetbegovic regime to hold out for more territory. Eventually the US manipulated a NATO bombing of Bosnia to defeat the Bosnian Serbs.

The Bosnian Serbs constituted about a third of the republic's population, with Muslims comprising 40 per cent and the Croats 18 per cent. In November 1991 the Bosnian Serbs held a referendum, in which votes cast were overwhelmingly against independence from Yugoslavia. Thus, when Bosnia-Hercegovina declared its independence in March 1992, the Republika Srpska or Serbian Republic of Bosnia-Hercegovina was declared under the leadership of Radovan Karadzic. Three and a half years of war ensued between the three component populations, during which the western media consistently and inaccurately portrayed Izetbegovic's rump government as the multi-ethnic victim of Serb aggression. The attempt was made to portray the war in Bosnia as the result of a Serbian invasion, rather than understanding it as a civil war where the Serbs had lived and worked on the land for 1,500 years and were defending their right to self-determination. In fact, Izetbegovic unconstitutionally asserted the right of his government to rule the whole of Bosnia-Hercegovina and sought western support to so do, even perpetuating the war in an attempt to secure western intervention to support his regime. The resulting war was brutal, with atrocities and ethnic cleansing carried out on all sides. The human suffering during the course of the war and the atrocities committed were terrible, yet this real suffering was exploited and manipulated for political ends to demonize the Serbian community. Successful attempts were made by Izetbegovic's regime – which employed a US-based PR firm – to give the impression that atrocities were conducted only by the Serbs, whereas all sides were responsible. The scale of atrocities was also massively inflated for political effect during the course of the war. While estimates of war dead were sometimes set as high as 200,000 to 300,000 by Izetbegovic's government, most informed estimates now suggest an upper limit of 35,000. Izetbegovic's government also suggested that up to 30,000 women had been raped, which rightly caused intense international outcry and condemnation. The Serbs were accused of being primarily responsible for these appalling crimes and of having a systematic policy of mass rape, organizing 'rape camps' for that purpose. Evidence does not seem to bear this out, however. A UN report concluded that a total of approximately 2,400 rapes had taken place, committed by all sides in the conflict.

In June 1992 the UN imposed economic sanctions on Yugoslavia, although the JNA was not formally supporting the Bosnian Serbs. By 1993 Milosevic was pressurizing the Bosnian Serbs to accept peace terms and by August 1994 had imposed an economic blockade on them. In October international sanctions against Yugoslavia were partially lifted following the admission of monitors to the Serbian–Bosnian border. Subsequently, in August 1995 Milosevic failed to support the Krajina Serbs and they were defeated by overwhelming Croatian forces, re-armed and trained by the United States and Germany. Some 300,000 Croatian-Serb refugees fled to Yugoslavia. This Croatian victory, combined with massive NATO bombing of Bosnian Serb targets, forced the Bosnian Serbs to accept peace negotiations, where they reluctantly accepted representation by Milosevic. These negotiations resulted in the Dayton

Accords, where Milosevic made a number of concessions, most significantly giving up the Serb claim on the Serb suburbs of the Bosnian capital, Sarajevo, which had been the power base of Radovan Karadzic.

The Dayton Accords resulted in a Bosnia that was effectively without sovereignty, divided under NATO occupation and under western colonial administration. Bosnia is run by the High Representative of the US and EU, who, like the IMF-appointed governor of the Bosnian Central Bank, may not be a citizen of Bosnia or a neighbouring state. The European Bank of Reconstruction and Development runs the Commission on Public Corporations which supervises the operations of all public services and their restructuring – in other words, privatization. Thus, while the west talks of its commitment to democracy, in fact actual power in Bosnia lies in the hands of non-elected, non-citizens acting in the interests of western creditors and investors.

THE QUESTION OF ISLAM

The population of Bosnia-Hercegovina was the most nationally complex of all the Yugoslav republics: 'in only 32 of Bosnia-Hercegovina's 109 districts did one of the three ethnic groups constitute 70 percent or more of the local population'.[2] It was, therefore, a great beneficiary of the multi-national ethos of Yugoslavia. The communities had a good track record of relations, as Ramet observes: 'Muslims, Serbs and Croats had lived in peace for most of the five hundred years they cohabited in Bosnia-Hercegovina.' It was true that there was inter-communal violence during the Second World War, but the conflict was primarily political rather than national. Indeed, as Ramet points out: 'Muslims and Croats ... were found in the ranks of both the Ustase and the Communist-led Partisans, while Serbs were found with both Draza Mihailovic's Chetniks and Tito's Partisans.'[3] The republic had the most to lose from any supposedly ethnic break-up of Yugoslavia, because the different nationalities were so integrated. In championing Bosnian recognition, the US lent its support to Bosnia's ruling Muslim faction, under the leadership of Alija Izetbegovic, generally portraying them as the innocent victims of primarily Serb aggression. Warren Zimmerman, US Ambassador to Yugoslavia, described Izetbegovic as 'mild-mannered, deferential and perpetually anxious; he wore the mantle of leadership with great discomfort. A devout Muslim but no extremist, he consistently advocated the preservation of a multinational Bosnia.'[4] This was not an accurate representation of the situation, and Izetbegovic was far from innocent of responsibility, as he had played a key role in the generation of Muslim nationalism, and – encouraged by the US – had pulled back from negotiated settlements with the Serb and Croat parties, hoping that the west would intervene on his behalf. All communities suffered as a result.

The Muslim community in Bosnia-Hercegovina is not ethnically different from the Serbian and Croatian communities. The Bosnian Muslims are the descendants of slavs who converted to Islam during the Ottoman period and there is also a large community of Macedonian Muslims who converted during the Ottoman period. These communities, which speak Serbo-Croat, are distinct from the – largely Muslim – Albanian communities in Yugoslavia or former Yugoslav republics. In 1971, they were constitutionally recognized as one of the 'nations' of Yugoslavia and comprised around 9 per cent of the overall population of Yugoslavia. In Bosnia-Hercegovina they were the largest national grouping, making up around 40 per cent of the population by the end of the 1980s. The Muslim community has a higher concentration in urban areas, and tends to be more prosperous than either of the other two main communities in Bosnia-Hercegovina, which are more predominantly rural-based. This has led US author and columnist William Pfaff to observe: 'There is a marked element of class war in today's "ethnic" war in Bosnia-Hercegovina.'[5]

After the break-up of the Ottoman Empire, the Muslim slavs formed the National Muslim Organization to defend their religious and cultural interests, but did not, on the whole, play a major role in politics in the inter-war years. In the immediate post-Second World War period, the Mladi Muslimani (Young Muslims) organization was founded, as Hugh Poulton observes, 'ostensibly to protect Muslims in Bosnia from alleged ill-treatment by the communist partisans. The Yugoslav authorities outlawed this group which they described as a terrorist one.'[6] One of the members of this group was Alija Izetbegovic.

On the whole the Muslim community in Bosnia did not have a high level of religious practice; indeed, religious believers in Bosnia-Hercegovina overall were lower, at 17 per cent, than in most other republics. In fact, the increasing sense of Muslim identity, which developed from the 1960s onwards, was as much oriented around cultural and social patterns as religious ones. According to East and Pontin: 'By the 1980s, the most salient such factors were a tendency to concentrate in urban areas, making them generally more educated, liberal and cosmopolitan than other ethnic groups in Bosnia-Hercegovina.'[7] Clearly, however, there were fundamentalist tendencies within the Muslim community, and this issue came to the fore in 1983, when 13 Muslims – including Izetbegovic – were accused of 'hostile and counter-revolutionary acts derived from Muslim nationalism'.[8]

The main charge concerned 'The Islamic Declaration', a 50-page exposition, written by Izetbegovic in 1970. The prosecution maintained that it supported the creation of a pure Muslim state, consisting of Bosnia-Hercegovina, Kosovo and other Muslim areas, and described it as 'the modernized platform of the former terrorist organization, the Young Muslims'.[9] Izetbegovic refuted the charges and stated that the Declaration referred to the emancipation of Muslims in general rather than in Yugoslavia specifically, and denied that he had called for an Islamic republic in Bosnia. According to Beloff, 'The Declaration ... takes a militantly Manichean view of the world. On the one side, Izetbegovic lauds the spiritually elevated Islamic world. On the other, he castigates the villainy of governments which have fallen under the corrupting Western influence. Such states also include not only those predominantly Christian but also Islamic states which have introduced a secular society.'[10] The Islamic Declaration was reprinted without changes for the 1990 election campaign.

Members of the group were also accused of having links with Khomeini in Iran after the revolution in 1979, and it has subsequently been alleged that since the mid-1980s, US Intelligence had been aware that Iran had been training 250 Bosnian Muslims each year. According to Gregory Copley, editor of *Strategic Policy*, Iran had a strategic objective in Bosnia, which was to support an Islamic state in Europe. It was certainly the case after Izetbegovic's Party of Democratic Action (SDA) was in government that a pan-Islamist approach emerged, and its leaders made visits to Islamic governments in the Middle East and Asia, seeking diplomatic and military support. In September 1992 'a pan-Islamic gathering in Zagreb called on all good Muslims to go to Bosnia and fight for the Bosnian Muslim cause'.[11]

In 1983 Izetbegovic was sentenced to 14 years in prison, which was reduced on appeal to 11 years, and he was actually released in November 1988, founding the SDA in May 1990. There were signs of a pan-Islamic approach from some elements within Yugoslavia's Muslim community during 1990. Slav Muslims from Montenegro formed a party with Albanians, which competed in the elections of that year. Of most concern to the Serbs, however, was support by Muslim groups for Albanian Kosovan separatism: according to Poulton: 'in February 1990, Muslim nationalist leaders supporting Kosovo's secession and attacking the Serb leader Slobodan Milosevic appeared in Novi Pazar in the Sandzak (part of Serbia)'.[12] In September 1990 further tensions occurred in Novibazar, when violence broke out at a rally held by Serbian opposition leader Vuk Draskovic. Draskovic accused Muslims of a closer affinity to Iran than to the Serbs, which led to fighting between Muslims and supporters of Draskovic's Serbian Renewal Movement. The apparent sympathy on the part of the SDA for Kosovan separatism was also a matter of considerable concern for the Serbian leadership, as was the SDA's announcement, after its electoral victory in 1990, that it would put more political effort into the Sanjak, as well as attempting to appeal to the Muslim Macedonians.

Izetbegovic's decision, in July 1991, to apply for Bosnian membership of the Organization of the Islamic Conference only served to compound these anxieties. It has also been suggested that Izetbegovic's regime was a radical Islamic regime tied closely to the Iran government, and to other Islamic groups, allegedly including Osama Bin Laden. Certainly, large amounts of material aid, such as food and medicines, were sent to Bosnia by Iran and Saudi Arabia, from 1992 onwards. Whatever the reality behind these more worrying suggestions, the US state department, under both Bush and Clinton administrations, brushed these concerns aside. However, in 1996 NATO raided terrorist training camps in Bosnia, which they found to have been run jointly by the Iranian and Bosnian governments.[13] Indeed, Ramet observes that 'clandestine weapons shipments to the Bosnian Muslims from Iran and other Islamic states began already in 1992, when George Bush was still U.S. president; the shipments were made with Croatian, but not

U.S. complicity, however, and the Croats skimmed a percentage off the top, including all heavy weaponry'.[14]

Thus it is, at the very least, clear that concerns about pan-Islamic tendencies amongst a small section of the Muslim population had real foundations, in the same way that concerns in Serbia about militant Kosovan Albanian secessionism and Greater Albanian nationalism were based on proven facts. In both cases, these were minority positions, but the crisis and destabilization in Yugoslav society in the 1980s, resulting from the economic reforms, exacerbated these problems. So too did foreign support for these positions, and greater numbers of people turned to support more extreme solutions.

THE BUILD-UP TO WAR

Tensions between the different communities in Bosnia-Hercegovina were apparent prior to the multi-party elections of November 1990, and they were exacerbated as nationalist political leaders sought to establish firm support for their parties. The result was that to a great extent voting patterns followed national lines. Discussions had already taken place between the leaders of Croatia and Serbia about the division of the republic, and then in March 1991 they also took place amongst the federal presidency about possible partition. In April, Bosnian Serbs on the border with Croatian Serb areas formed a regional parliament for Bosanska Krajina, and in June the supporters of the SDS in both Bosnia and Croatia signed a cooperation agreement. With the conclusion of the conflict in Slovenia, and therefore the beginning of the actual break-up of the federal state, one of the SDS representatives in the Bosnian presidency appealed to the JNA 'to "protect Serbs" in Bosnia'.[15]

In the summer of 1991 attempts were made to arrive at a negotiated settlement. Izetbegovic had indicated a desire to remain within a modified Yugoslav federation, and he participated in talks with the Bosnian Serbs and Milosevic, organized by Adil Zulfikarpasic of the moderate Muslim Bosniak Organization. Zulfikarpasic, together with SDS leader Radovan Karadzic, organized a number of mass inter-communal rallies, notably at Trebinje and Zvornik, urging peaceful coexistence between the communities, in support of these talks. The aim of these talks was a unitary republic in a revamped Yugoslavia. According to Norah Beloff, an agreement was being negotiated and Izetbegovic was apparently ready to sign, but then, following a trip to the United States, 'he dramatically demolished Zulfikarpasic's initiative. From July 1991, Izetbegovic and the SDA ran a hostile campaign, treating Zulfikarpasic as a traitor to the Muslim cause.'[16] By the middle of September fighting had spread from Croatia over the border into Bosnia-Hercegovina.

In mid-October, the Bosnian parliament debated a proposal on sovereignty put forward by Izetbegovic's SDA. It was supported by the SDA and Croatian HDZ, but strongly opposed by the Serbian SDS. Following the election in November 1990, these three parties had formed a coalition government, from which the SDS now withdrew to demonstrate its implacable opposition to the proposal for secession from Yugoslavia. It stressed that such a move would be unconstitutional without the agreement of all three communities, and emphasized that the Serbian community wished to remain within Yugoslavia. Later in October the SDS members of the Bosnian parliament declared themselves to be the parliament of the Bosnian Serbs. In November, the SDS held a referendum in Bosnian Serb areas, which voted overwhelmingly in favour of remaining within Yugoslavia. Simultaneously, Croatian HDZ leaders in Bosnia set up two autonomous Croatian areas in Bosnia-Hercegovina, recognizing the Bosnia government as long as it was independent from Yugoslavia. Not surprisingly, in November the Bosnian government asked the UN to supply peace-keeping forces, but the UN did not send such forces to areas which were still at peace. They had, however, extended the UN arms embargo on the republics – at Milosevic's request, in September 1991.

In December 1991 the rump Bosnian government (without the SDS) applied to the Badinter Commission for EC recognition of Bosnian independence; the following day the SDS announced its intention to establish a Bosnian Serb republic. As noted in the previous chapter, the Badinter Commission required the Bosnian government to hold a referendum to indicate majority support for independence. The Commission also ruled – essentially in line with the Bosnian constitution – that the referendum result would only be valid if there was positive support in all three communities. By this time the situation in Bosnia was deteriorating rapidly: 'Refugees from the fighting in Croatia (both Serb and Croat) had been flooding into northern Bosnia, villagers were arming (some with the aid of local territorial defense forces), and Croatia had sent armed forces to western Hercegovina.'[17] In fact, the Croatian government now intervened directly in Bosnian affairs by replacing the pro-Bosnian unity leader of the Bosnian HDZ with the strongly Croatian nationalist Mate Boban. Boban at once declared the Croat state of Herzeg-Bosna, in western Hercegovina. With the SDS out of government, and the Croats changing their line, the Bosnian government introduced emergency rule. This meant that the constitutionally required rotation of the Bosnian presidency, where each nation would take it in turns to supply the president, was abandoned.

The EC-required referendum on independence for Bosnia took place from 29 February to 1 March 1992, with a boycott by the Bosnian Serbs. Of eligible voters, 63.4 per cent took part, and of valid votes cast, 99.7 per cent voted for independence. The Badinter Commission's ruling on all-community participation was ignored, as was the constitution, which rendered this vote invalid because, under the constitution, such major changes required a consensus from all three national communities. On 3 March, Izetbegovic's rump government proclaimed the independence of Bosnia-Herce-govina. Having accelerated the republic on the road to war by engaging in the process towards recognition, the EC then made a considerable effort to find common ground between the three parties before recognition was granted. A conference on Bosnia-Hercegovina was set up, and Lord Carrington appointed the Portuguese minister, Cutileiro to negotiate between the parties. This attempt made good progress and, on 18 March, all three signed the resulting Lisbon Agreement. This agreed a republic of three constituent nations, each with the right to self-determination, and a regional cantonization on ethno-national lines. According to Lord Carrington, this was 'the last chance to try to preserve Bosnia before the war broke out in earnest'.[18]

While the Agreement accepted the framework of national division as a basis for the future Bosnia, rather than any consideration of 'a civil state based on individual rights',[19] it did open the way for a negotiated settlement. Had the Agreement been implemented, then it is possible that war would have been avoided. However, only days after signing it, Izetbegovic disavowed his signature, followed shortly afterwards by Mate Boban, the Croat representative. This change of mind by Izetbegovic took place after a meeting with the US Ambassador Warren Zimmerman, who acknowledged that Izetbegovic had signed in order to get EC recognition for Bosnia, even though he favoured a unitary state. Apparently, Zimmerman told Izetbegovic that if he didn't like the Agreement he should hold out for a unitary state.[20] Izetbegovic took this advice and pulled out of the Lisbon Agreement. This served to confirm the view that the US was now pursuing its own interests in Bosnia, and asserting them over what it perceived to be European interests, rather than seeking to prevent war. As Perry Anderson has observed: 'The US scuppered the Lisbon accords, preferring to dictate its own settlement in Bosnia, if necessary at the price of further ethnic cleansing, rather than accept an EU initiative.'[21] On 5 April the Bosnian government ordered 'a general mobilization of territorial defence forces and army reserves'.[22] Having brought down the Lisbon Agreement, on 6 April, the US succeeded in pressurizing the EC into recognition of Bosnia before an effective political settlement was in place. Thus war was assured.

This step, as Woodward observes, 'eliminated the last hope of a comprehensive settlement – such as an association of the remaining four Yugoslav states with some confederal relationship with Croatia – that could prevent further war'.[23] In Woodward's view, the purpose of the recognition of Croatia for Germany, and Bosnia-Hercegovina for the US, was to appease the domestic Croatian lobby, boost their foreign ministers, and assert themselves within the Euro-Atlantic Alliance. The latter point is the strongest one, for the newly reunited Germany was flexing its muscles and establishing a sphere of influence in central Europe through the recognition of Croatia – which it had pressed ahead and done in spite of US opposition. Having lost its previous goal of establishing an effectively free-market, IMF-controlled Yugoslavia under Markovic, the US had then to rethink its strategy towards Yugoslavia, and opted to shape and control the future Bosnia. In Izetbegovic the US found a willing ally who pulled back from the Lisbon compromise and headed for recognition or bust – and thus war – in the baggage car of US geostrategic interests.

THE WAR BEGINS

On 1 March, the day the referendum was completed, two Muslim and one Croat gunman attacked a Serbian Orthodox wedding party in Sarajevo. The priest was wounded and the groom's father was killed. The following day, Serb roadblocks were set up in Sarajevo and the Serbs demanded either that there should be Serb police in Serb areas of Sarajevo, or that it should become a UN protectorate. Nevertheless, Izetbegovic went ahead and declared independence, by which time, according to Ramet, the Bosnian Serb leader, Radovan Karadzic was talking of war to keep Bosnian Serb areas part of Yugoslavia.[24] By early April open conflict had broken out, and on 6 April Bosnian Serb forces, backed by the JNA, began to consolidate control over the Bosnian Serb areas. By the middle of May Serb forces had achieved this, establishing control in over 60 per cent of the republic, largely the areas in which Serbs had resided for hundreds of years. As General Charles G. Boyd has pointed out, with regard to both Croatia and Bosnia:

> Much of what Zagreb calls the occupied territories is in fact land held by Serbs for more than three centuries, ever since imperial Austria moved Serbs to the frontier (the Krajina) to protect the shopkeepers of Vienna (and Zagreb) from the Ottomans. The same is true of most Serb land in Bosnia, what the Western media frequently refers to as the 70% of Bosnia seized by rebel Serbs. There were only 500,000 fewer Serbs than Muslims in Bosnia at independence, with the more rural Serbs tending towards larger landholdings. In short the Serbs are not trying to conquer new territory, but merely to hold on to what was already theirs.[25]

Under considerable international pressure, on 20 May Milosevic ordered the demobilization of the JNA, which became the VJ (Army of Yugoslavia) and non-Bosnian Serb troops withdrew from the republic. All three parties to the conflict inherited JNA weaponry, and a considerable number of troops – particularly of Bosnian origin – were transferred to the new Army of the Serbian Republic of Bosnia-Hercegovina, under the command of Ratko Mladic. By the end of 1992 the Bosnian Serb forces had consolidated their area of control in 70 per cent of the republic.

The western powers were slow to act in the face of this war, however, largely because they had differing interests and supported different parties in the conflict. The US was backing Izetbegovic's regime, but wanted to leave any intervention to the Europeans; Germany and Austria supported Croatia, and France and Russia were more sympathetic to Serbia. Britain did not have a strong position. International action began to take place under the auspices of the United Nations. At the beginning of June 1992 the

UN imposed trade sanctions on the Federal Republic of Yugoslavia (as the federation of the republics of Serbia and Montenegro now was called). This did not have a negative impact only on Yugoslavia, however. According to Misha Glenny, other Balkan countries and Hungary objected to the sanctions regime because of the central role that Serbia played for them both commercially and in terms of overland trading routes: 'although sanctions gave the international community a certain leverage in its diplomatic dealings with Belgrade, they also encouraged economic decline throughout the whole region'.[26] Also in early June, the UN Security Council authorized a UN Protection Force (UNPROFOR) of 1,000 peace-keepers to take over Sarajevo airport. From that base, UNPROFOR quickly increased in size in the republic in the subsequent months, to 17,000 by 1995. In August 1992 the EC convened the London Conference, which recognized the territorial integrity of Bosnia-Hercegovina, and identified Yugoslavia as the aggressor. It also called for UN peace-keeping forces to be sent to the republic, to guarantee a cease-fire.

In September 1992 the Geneva Peace Conference, under the leadership of Lord Owen, on behalf of the EC, and Cyrus Vance on behalf of the UN, began to look for ways of negotiating a peaceful settlement. Sabrina Ramet has criticized Owen and Vance for, as she describes it, repudiating the mandate from the London Conference. Instead of honouring, as Ramet sees it, the London Conference's recognition of

> the elected government of Alija Izetbegovic as having, by that virtue, a status higher than that of insurgent forces, Vance and Owen introduced the notion of 'three warring factions'. This placed the government of Sarajevo on the same level with the Croat and Serbian insurgents.[27]

Clearly Vance and Owen had a better understanding than Ramet of the constitution of Bosnia-Hercegovina, and the fact that the republic comprised three constituent nations, all of whose consent was required for major changes to take place. Vance and Owen were quite right to have a conception of negotiating between the three Bosnian communities on an equal basis. Ramet deplores Vance and Owen's 'decision to reward Serb aggression', by discussing the partition of Bosnia-Hercegovina, but clearly she has overlooked the fact that the Serbs were constitutionally entitled to self-determination, whereas Izetbegovic's rump government was not constitutionally entitled to declare Bosnia-Hercegovina independent.

The Vance–Owen Plan proposed the division of Bosnia-Hercegovina into ten ethnic cantons. The proposal was accepted by the Bosnian Croats and ultimately by Izetbegovic, but rejected by the Bosnian Serbs in January 1993. In April 1993 the EC declared that, if the Bosnian Serbs and Yugoslavia did not accept the Vance–Owen Plan, they would be isolated and ostracized. Shortly thereafter the UN Security Council called for a strengthening of economic sanctions against Yugoslavia. Milosevic supported the Vance–Owen Plan, and attempted to persuade Karadzic to support it also. Although Karadzic himself was persuaded to sign it in May 1993, the Bosnian Serb Assembly subsequently refused to endorse it. Milosevic strongly condemned the Bosnian Serbs for this, and refused to supply them with any further military support, although food and medical supplies were still forthcoming. The Vance–Owen Plan was now abandoned and Lord Owen began, on behalf of the EC, to recommence negotiations.

Although in the first phase of the Bosnian war there was an alliance between the Croats and Muslims, this broke down in April 1993, when the Bosnian Croats attempted to occupy lands that would have come to them under the Vance–Owen Plan. In June 1993 Serbs and Croats achieved a stand-off, and came up with a joint plan for the partition of the republic, while Croatian and Muslim forces were now engaged in warfare. Lord Owen, with his new UN counterpart, Thorvald Stoltenberg, then came up with the Owen–Stoltenberg Plan in August 1993. This Plan gave 52 per cent of the republic to the Bosnian Serbs, 30 per cent to the Muslims and 18 per cent to the Croats. This was agreed by the Croats and Serbs, and in July 1993 the Muslims agreed to the Plan in principle, although conflict continued while negotiations took place on the details. It subsequently became apparent that the US was encouraging the Muslims to hold out for more.

Some of the most widely watched events of the war were those that took place in Sarajevo from April 1992 to February 1994, where the conflict was usually described as a 'siege' by the Serbs. In fact, Sarajevo was a divided city, with established battle lines and the Serb and Muslim communities tragically fighting each other. UN General Lewis MacKenzie criticized the Bosnian Serb forces for using heavy artillery in areas of Sarajevo, but he also observed that most of the

19 cease-fires that he negotiated were broken by Muslim forces, who wanted the west to intervene.[28] Indeed, the UN documented and reported that Bosnian government forces mortared the airport – a position corroborated by Lord Owen, who wrote in his book, *Balkan Odyssey*, that Muslim forces would from time to time shell the airport to stop relief flights, in order to focus world attention on Sarajevo.[29] Other non-Serb participants have made similar observations – for example, French General Philippe Morillon, former commander of UNPROFOR, 'charged that the Bosnian government repeatedly refused to let UNPROFOR establish a ceasefire because it wanted to keep Sarajevo a focal point for world sympathy'.[30] In addition, General Sir Michael Rose, 'came to the same conclusion, noting in his memoir that the Muslim deputy commander was reluctant to sign the ceasefire even though "the Serbs had agreed to all of his government's ceasefire demands"'.[31] Incidences of Muslim forces attacking friendly targets, or shooting Muslim civilians, in order to blame the Serbs, were not uncommon, including the 'infamous breadline and marketplace massacres in Sarajevo, in 1992, 1994, and 1995. In all three incidents internal UN investigations revealed that Bosnian Muslim forces were responsible.'[32] As General Charles G. Boyd commented: 'no seasoned observer in Sarajevo doubts for a moment that Muslim forces have found it in their interest to shell friendly targets'.[33] Indeed, the UN protested at the Bosnian government orchestrating incidents to set up the Serbs – often provoking them to retaliation, which would then be recorded by the world's media.[34]

The Bosnian Serbs consistently lost the media and public relations battle, which was a notable feature of the break-up of Yugoslavia. Both the Croats and the Izetbegovic regime employed US public relations companies, and the Serbs were much less adept in this area, although of course much of the western media was already predisposed to assume Serbian guilt. There were a number of examples where Serbs were on the receiving end of extreme violence, which were not widely reported, and others where reprehensible Serb behaviour was mirrored in the other communities, but all sides were not reported. As US General Charles G. Boyd, who was Deputy Commander in Chief of the US European Command from November 1992 to July 1995, observed in the autumn of 1995, recently more than 90 per cent of the Serbs in western Slavonia were ethnically cleansed when Croatian troops overran that U.N.-protected area in May. As of this writing this Croatian operation appears to differ from Serbian actions around the U.N. safe areas of Srebrenica and Zepa only in the degree of Western hand-wringing and CNN footage the latter have elicited. Ethnic cleansing evokes condemnation only when it is committed by Serbs, not against them.[35]

There were numerous other examples. In June 1992, the Serbs were virtually eliminated in Mostar in violent attacks by Croat and Muslim forces, but this did not get fully aired. Serbian atrocities in Srebrenica in 1995 – including the alleged massacre of over 7,000 Muslim men and boys – were widely publicized, although it is notable that by the end of the 1990s only a tiny fraction of the anticipated number of bodies had been found. The fact that Serbs had previously been brutally driven out of Srebrenica by the Muslim leader Oric, and had suffered atrocities at Muslim hands – such as the massacre of 500 Serb civilians on the Orthodox Christmas Eve in 1993 – were not widely reported. Media coverage of the Serb detention camp at Omarska did much to horrify western public opinion and turn it against the Serbs, yet brutal detention camps run by the Croats at Detlj and by Izetbegovic's regime in Konic were not equally reported and condemned. In fact, the Commander of Omarska camp was taken to the UN War Crimes Tribunal, but the charges against him were subsequently dropped. This suggests that the accusations made against the Serbs were on occasion inflated. For example, a major US intelligence report concluded that, while serious abuses had taken place on the part of the Serbs, there was no evidence of organized mass killing. Indeed, the International Committee of the Red Cross reported: 'Serbs, Croats and Muslims all run detention camps and must share equal blame.'[36]

It should be noted, however, that not all Muslims were united behind Izetbegovic's government. Under the leadership of Fikret Abdic, who had been a member of the Bosnian collective presidency, the Autonomous Province of Western Bosnia was declared in the Bihac region. Abdic concluded peace and cooperation agreements with both Bosnian Serbs and Bosnian Croatians, fighting Izetbe-govic's forces throughout the war, 'until the war's final days, when

NATO's aerial attacks allowed Izetbegovic's troops to take huge chunks of territory from both the Bosnian Serbs and Abdic'.[37]

One of the main concerns of Izetbegovic's government was to get the arms embargo lifted, but despite efforts by the US – supported by Islamic countries – in the UN Security Council in June 1993, this was not forthcoming. However, the US persisted in its support of Izetbegovic's government and began to develop plans for aerial bombardment of the Bosnian Serbs. They were, however, resistant to British and French calls for the US to send troops to join the UN peace-keeping forces. At the beginning of August 1993 the US tried to get NATO agreement for air strikes but, eventually, support was tied to UN agreement. Yasushi Akashi, responsible for the UN forces in Bosnia, put his authority to use, according to Ramet, 'by repeatedly (although not consistently) vetoing NATO requests to conduct punitive strikes against the Serbs'.[38] The US also pursued its military interests in the region by concluding a military assistance agreement with Albania in October 1993.

Further US intervention in early 1994 resulted in improved relations between the Croats and Muslims. In March 1994 the Washington Agreement was concluded, creating a Muslim–Croat federation, in alliance against the Serbs – which was now increasingly well armed. According to Ramet, 'on 27 April 1994, U.S. President Clinton approved a policy of turning a blind eye to Iranian arms shipments to Croatia and Bosnia, keeping the decision quiet at the time'.[39] These developments led Izetbegovic's forces to launch an offensive against the Bosnian Serbs in the early summer of 1994, but by July this offensive had been defeated.

The UN and EU now came up with another proposal for the partition of Bosnia, offering 51 per cent to the Croat–Muslim federation, and 49 per cent to the Bosnian Serbs. This was again rejected by the Bosnian Serb assembly, against the advice of Milosevic, who then closed Yugoslav borders to arms traffic to Bosnia.

By September Bosnian Muslim forces were beginning to make some headway, since they were not only considerably larger numerically than the Bosnian Serb forces, but they were also being increasingly well armed from foreign sources. The United States was lobbying hard for military action against the Bosnian Serbs. Indeed, on 28 September, US Defence Secretary William Perry said 'that he wanted NATO to use "compelling force" against Bosnian Serb forces',[40] although the British and French remained opposed.

The US now began a unilateral intervention in Bosnia with the intention of defeating the Serbs and supporting the Muslim–Croat forces. In October the US announced that it was sending a military mission to Sarajevo to help train the Muslim–Croat forces for combat, with the Pentagon planning to provide up to $5 billion worth of weaponry to Izetbegovic's regime. At the end of November the US signed an agreement on military cooperation with Croatia, including US military training for Croatia's armed forces. In December former US president Jimmy Carter successfully negotiated a 4-month cease-fire, which included an exchange of prisoners between the Bosnian Serbs and Izetbegovic's regime. By spring 1995, however, both the Croatian army and Izetbegovic's forces were significantly strengthened in weaponry, training and morale and heavy fighting resumed towards the end of March.

THE FINAL STAGES

On 1 May 1995 the Croatian army crossed the UN cease-fire lines and attacked the Serb community in western Slavonia. The following day the Croats declared that they had 'liberated' 1,000 square kilometres of Croatian land and a mass exodus of Serbs followed. On 4 August, in Operation Storm, US-trained Croatian forces attacked Knin, the capital of the Krajina, taking it and most of the Krajina within a few days. This led to many deaths and a massive population flight of up to 300,000 Serbs to Bosnian Serb territories and into Yugoslavia. As Ramet observes, 'as a result of this campaign, the Serbian presence in Croatia, which had accounted for about 12 percent of the republic's population in 1991, was reduced to a mere 3 percent'.[41] This was the largest example of ethnic cleansing during the break-up of Yugoslavia.

In May, NATO bombing attacks on weapons dumps near Pale led the Bosnian Serbs to turn against the UN and NATO. As Momcilo Krajisnik, chair of the Bosnian Serb parliament stated: 'with this attack NATO and the UN have finally buried their impartiality and destroyed our trust in them'.[42] UN personnel were then taken as hostages by the Bosnian Serb forces, but released in mid-June under pressure from Yugoslavia. UN personnel were now withdrawn from Bosnian Serb-held areas.

In July the Bosnian Serbs took the UN 'safe havens' of Srebrenica and Zepa. The US government now proposed a massive stepping-up of the sporadic NATO bombing that had been taking place since 1993, and the French and British agreed. Russia objected, but her protestations were ignored. Units of NATO's Rapid Reaction Force under British and French command were also deployed on the ground. NATO issued a warning to the Bosnian Serbs that, if they attempted to take Gorazde or any other UN 'safe havens', this would meet with a decisive response. The UN began withdrawing its personnel from Gorazde in August, but in fact the bombardment began after a mortar attack in Sarajevo was attributed to Bosnian Serb forces. In the event, a French and British investigation determined that the shell came from Muslim-held positions in Sarajevo.[43] Nevertheless, this was used as the trigger for two days of intensive NATO bombing of Bosnian Serb targets, which began on 30 August. Attacks ceased temporarily on 1 September, but in the absence of a Bosnian Serb capitulation, they recommenced on 5 September in spite of Russian protests. On 16 September, after over a week of heavy bombing, the Bosnian Serbs began to comply with a UN deadline and withdrew heavy weaponry from Sarajevo. Simultaneously, Croat and Muslim troops launched attacks on Bosnian Serb areas. Fighting continued for some weeks until peace talks were finally convened at the Wright-Patterson Air Force Base in Dayton, Ohio on 1 November 1995.

THE DAYTON ACCORDS

The key players in the discussions were Tudjman, Milosevic and Izetbegovic. Milosevic represented both Yugoslavia and the Bosnian Serbs, since Karadzic and Mladic had by now both been indicted on war crimes charges. On 21 November the agreement was concluded, recognizing Bosnia-Hercegovina as a sovereign state comprised of two entities, the Muslim–Croat Federation, with 51 per cent of territory, and the Bosnian Serb Republic, with 49 per cent. It was agreed that Bosnia-Hercegovina would have an elected collective presidency and parliament based in Sarajevo and a single monetary system. Sarajevo was to be under the control of the Federation and a land corridor was to link it with Gorazde. Srebrenica and Zepa were to remain under Serb control. Citizens were guaranteed freedom of movement within Bosnia-Hercegovina and the right to return to their properties and reclaim their assets. Indicted war criminals were excluded from office.

The Accords were signed in Paris on 14 December and a programme for withdrawal of forces and exchange of territory was agreed. I-FOR, the 60,000 strong NATO-commanded implementation force, was set up to implement the agreements, replacing UNPROFOR which withdrew at the end of January 1996. 'I-For was given complete freedom of movement and the tasks of resettling refugees, settling border disputes, and establishing "secure conditions" for free elections. I-For commanders were given strong powers to control communications and regulate military movements.'[44]

There was strong hostility towards the agreement from the Bosnian Serb community, although Karadzic promised that it would be implemented in full. The main bone of contention was that the Agreement handed over control of the Serb-majority suburbs of Sarajevo – which were Karadzic's main base of support – to the Federation. Anger directed at Milosevic for agreeing to this deal was considerable. In December, 98 per cent of Sarajevo's 120,000 Serb community voted against the agreement.

Under the Dayton Accords the role of international supervision was key in the development of the Bosnian state. A transitional international administration was organized to run the country until the first general elections in September 1996, but in fact that administration continued subsequent to the elections. The powers of the central state authorities were extremely limited, 'even to the extent of excluding central control over the armed forces, while wide-ranging powers over government institutions were to be given to internationally appointed individuals for between five and six years'.[45] International involvement was written into the Bosnian constitution – for example, it states that the first Governor of the Central Bank will be appointed by the IMF and may not be a citizen of Bosnia or a neighbouring state. The entire process of democratization and reconstruction was to be organized by the foreign nominees of the OSCE, IMF, UN and similar international institutions. Legislative and executive power resides with the UN High Representative, initially Carl Bildt the former Swedish prime minister, followed by Carlos Westendorp of Spain and in summer 2002 by former British Liberal Party leader, Lord Ashdown.

The UN High Representative has the right to over-rule the governments of both the Federation and Republika Srpska. As Lord

Ashdown has said: 'What we have now is near imperialism. We need to move from a quasi-protectorate to something more acceptable.'[46]

This post-Dayton process has given rise to considerable debate and criticism of the arrangements in Bosnia, and in the view of Michel Chossudovsky, 'a full-fledged colonial administration' has been installed.[47] Certainly, the western institutions have been extremely interventionist in their approach to post-Dayton Bosnia. As Chossudovsky puts it starkly: 'With a Bosnian peace settlement holding under NATO guns, the west unveiled a "reconstruction" program which fully stripped Bosnia-Herzegovina of its economic and political sovereignty. This program largely consists in developing Bosnia-Herzegovina as a divided territory under NATO military occupation and Western administration.'[48]

8
War: the third wave – Kosovo

The war in Bosnia was brought to a conclusion by the military intervention of NATO, under the leadership of the United States. It was also the United States that played the major role in bringing about the NATO bombing of Yugoslavia in 1999, ostensibly over the treatment of the Kosovan Albanians. The war was portrayed as a conflict between Serbs and Kosovan Albanians, with the west conducting a humanitarian intervention on behalf of the latter, to secure their safety and self-determination. In fact, the US had decided to defeat Milosevic, who was obstructing the full integration of Yugoslavia into the western institutional framework. The legitimate grievances of the Kosovan Albanians were manipulated by the west and used to justify the attempts to destroy the remaining parts of the socialist economy of Yugoslavia in order to fully open up the region to capitalist expansion. The real conflict, therefore, was between the US-led NATO and the Yugoslav state. As NATO commander General Wesley K. Clark described the war: 'It was coercive diplomacy, the use of armed forces to impose the political will of the NATO nations on the Federal Republic of Yugoslavia, or more specifically, on Serbia.'[1]

The war against Yugoslavia also presented an opportunity for NATO – in which the US was pre-eminent – to redefine itself in the post-Cold War framework. The first wave of NATO expansion, the negotiations for which were concluded just days before the NATO bombardment began, had taken NATO into the former socialist bloc, enlisting Hungary, Poland and the Czech Republic. A successful war against Yugoslavia, would have two useful results: first, NATO would not need to tolerate the existence of a 'rogue' state like Yugoslavia in its 'strategic underbelly'; and second, NATO would, as former White House official Peter W. Rodman pointed out, demonstrate

> its relevance and effectiveness in the new era by combating ethnic violence in Europe. No other institution – neither the United Nations, not the European Union (EU), nor the Organi-

zation for Security and Cooperation in Europe – was capable of military heavy lifting. A success in Kosovo … would guarantee the primacy of NATO in Europe's future. There would be no doubt that NATO was the pre-eminent and indispensable security institution on the continent.[2]

The problems of Kosovo required a political not a military solution, as was indeed the line pursued by the elected representatives of the Kosovan Albanians, like Ibrahim Rugova of the Democratic League of Kosovo (LDK). The pre-eminence of peaceful campaigning was only superseded when western interests began to fund the very marginal terrorist secessionist group, the Kosovo Liberation Army (KLA). From 1996, the KLA embarked on a violent campaign against the Kosovan police, aimed at provoking them into a violent response, which eventually did draw such an armed response to KLA strongholds from Yugoslav government forces. An OSCE verification mission entered Kosovo, but the United States attempted to force what would in effect be a NATO occupation of the whole of Yugoslavia onto the Yugoslav government, via the Rambouillet Accords. The Yugoslav government refused to sign the Accords and the NATO bombardment of Yugoslavia began. The bombardment was illegal under international law, as Yugoslavia was a sovereign state with internationally recognized borders, and such an unsolicited intervention in the internal affairs of a sovereign state was excluded by international law. Although justified by its proponents as a humanitarian war, the NATO intervention contravened the UN charter and was outside NATO's own remit as a defensive organization of its member states. In fact, far from solving a supposed humanitarian crisis, the bombardment led to the flight of hundreds of thousands of Kosovans, primarily to Albania and Macedonia, actually *causing* a humanitarian crisis. The bombardment also caused the deaths of many innocent civilians and resulted in serious damage to the social and economic infrastructure of Yugoslavia. On conclusion of the war, rather than self-determination being achieved, Kosovo became a UN/NATO protectorate.

THE KLA AND THE MOVE TOWARDS WAR

While the vast majority of the Kosovan Albanian population supported the pacifist approach to securing independence, espoused by Ibrahim Rugova, there had for some time existed a number of small groups of secessionists prepared to take a more radical path. These groups were often based abroad, in Germany or Switzerland,[3] or other countries with Albanian *Gastarbeiter* communities, where militant secessionists had fled in the 1980s. Some of these exiles founded the Popular Movement for Kosovo in 1982, arguing that 'Kosovo would only achieve freedom through an armed uprising.'[4] In the early 1990s they played a crucial part in founding the KLA. The KLA were, however, relatively marginal to the political process in Kosovo until 1998. Rugova had declared Kosovan independence in 1990 – although no country had recognized it – and in 1992 the province had held its own parallel state elections, unrecognized by the Serbian government, in which Rugova was elected president. A number of factors helped to change this situation, however. According to James Pettifer, 'The leadership of Ibrahim Rugova was fatally compromised by the autumn 1995 Dayton Accords, which delivered nothing to the Kosovars ... and after Dayton more and more Kosovars turned to radical paths of political thought and action.'[5] In particular, the EU states subsequently recognized the territorial integrity of Yugoslavia, indicating that the Kosovan Albanians could not hope to achieve European support for their independence. While the lack of progress at Dayton did constitute a great disappointment, in fact, however, support for the KLA amongst the Kosovan Albanian population never rose above 15–20 per cent, and the overwhelming majority continued to support Rugova.

The crucial factor in the shifting fortunes of the KLA was international support, especially from the US. A significant indication of US interest in Kosovo occurred in 1996, when it established a government presence in Pristina in the form of a US Information Agency cultural centre – described by former US Ambassador to the UN, Richard Holbrooke, as 'a virtual US embassy'.[6] Yet, even before the US adopted the KLA and made it into a political actor on the international stage, covert support for the KLA had been forthcoming from the BND, the German Secret Service. As Retired Admiral Elmar Schmahling of German Military Counter-Intelligence has observed: 'The German Secret Service played a very important role in supporting terrorist groups in Serbia.'[7] Indeed, BND operatives trained KLA fighters, picked their officers and gave them weapons.[8] The KLA also secured considerable amounts of weaponry after the fall of the Albanian government in the spring of 1997. The collapse of a pyramid scheme left huge numbers of people destitute, resulting in a popular armed uprising in which government weapons stores were looted.

The KLA were portrayed by their western backers as 'classic Balkan rebels', the underdogs fighting against Serbian oppression,[9] but this image – perhaps created by the US company Ruder Finn which allegedly handled their public relations[10] – did not square with reality. In April 1996 the KLA began a series of assassinations of civilians and police within Kosovo, and terrorized Serbs and other minorities within the province. According to Parenti, between 1996 and 1998 over half the KLA's victims were Albanians perceived to be 'collaborators': those who did not support the KLA, who were members of the Socialist Party, or were loyal in some way to the Yugoslav state. 'The KLA assassinated Albanians who were employed in Serbian or FRY public services, including police inspectors, forest service workers, postal employees, and public utility workers.'[11] Not surprisingly, the Yugoslav government described the KLA as a terrorist organization – a description with which there was widespread agreement. Even in 1998 US officials were referring to the KLA as a terrorist organization. For example, Robert Gelbard, US special envoy to Bosnia said: 'We condemn very strongly terrorist actions in Kosovo. The UCK [KLA] is without any question a terrorist group.'[12] The KLA was also widely recognized as being involved with the drugs trade, it being noted by the US Drug Enforcement Administration in 1995 that separatist activities in Kosovo were being funded in this way.

Eventually, the KLA attacks on civilians and police in Kosovo, to which the Serbian police had responded in an ad hoc fashion, drew an armed response from the Yugoslav government forces and in the summer of 1998 they organized a concerted offensive against KLA strongholds. Despite having previously characterized the KLA as terrorists, the US administration now threatened to bomb Yugoslavia unless the government agreed to withdraw its forces from the province, verified by an OSCE mission. Madeline Albright, US Secretary of State, appeared to be eager for a confrontation with Milosevic and urged President Clinton to bomb the Serbs.[13] Holbrooke went to meet Milosevic and the KLA. An agreement was reached on 13 October 1998, and over 1,000 OSCE verifiers went to Kosovo to oversee the withdrawal of government troops. A de-escalation of tension began, although there were some outbursts

of violence, usually instigated by the KLA.[14] For a while the presence
of the OSCE mission had a calming effect on the province. As Rollie
Keith of the Kosovo Verification Mission observed:

> We had an opportunity, imperfect as it was, to work and to
> monitor and to seek a rational, logical, civil solution to the
> problems and the grievances within Kosovo. Kosovo was a political
> problem that could not be solved by bombing from 23,000 feet.
> This had to be solved by negotiations and diplomacy.[15]

However, as Judah points out, 'as the Serbs pulled back, the KLA
advanced to fill the vacuum'.[16] The KLA was not intending to give
up the armed struggle for Kosovan independence, or incorporation into a Greater Albania (the unification of all ethnic Albanians
in the region into an enlarged Albanian state), and from January
the KLA recommenced its military provocation of the Yugoslav
authorities. In January 1999 a supposed massacre of Kosovan
Albanian civilians by Yugoslav government forces took place at
Racak. Head of the OSCE Verification Mission, William Walker – a
former US Ambassador to El Salvador who had been criticized for
his close relations with the military government there – was at the
scene almost immediately. Walker asserted that the deaths at Racak
were the result of a massacre, but many observers at the time were
unconvinced by the scene, and independent autopsy evidence
showed that they were most likely fighters killed in combat and put
in place later by the KLA to resemble a massacre. Racak was used
by the US to justify a further stage in the process that would rapidly
lead to the bombing of Yugoslavia – the talks at Rambouillet.

RAMBOUILLET AND THE LEGALITY OF THE ATTACK

In February 1999, talks were convened in Rambouillet, in France,
to resolve the Kosovo issue. Delegations participated from the
Yugoslav government, the KLA and the EU and US – headed by
Madeline Albright. By this time, the US had revised their earlier
view of the KLA as terrorists, and now accorded them the status of
national leaders, encouraging and promoting them internationally. As James Pettifer observes: 'Around the time of the Rambouillet
conference ... the KLA underwent a visible change. Its leaders
became public figures and they formed a government in exile in
Tirana, locked in fierce competition with the earlier government

in exile headed by LDK's Bujar Bukoshi.'[17] The US had clearly decided to back the KLA and sideline Rugova, whom one might have expected to lead the Kosovan delegation. In fact, it was the 28-year-old KLA military commander Hashim Thaci – newly designated the KLA's prime-minister in exile – who took the leading position, and Rugova was his deputy.

The text produced by Albright was acceptable to neither the Yugoslav nor the Kosovan delegations. It provided for 30,000 NATO troops in Kosovo, a referendum on Kosovan independence after three years, Kosovan Albanian control of 28 out of 31 police districts, and 2,500 VJ troops and 1,500 Serbian police in the province. It also included in Appendix B, what amounted to the right of NATO forces to have free range throughout the whole of Yugoslavia. The Kosovan delegation did not wish to accept a 3-year delay on independence, but were pressurized by Albright into accepting the text. The Yugoslav delegation was, however, absolutely unwilling to accept Appendix B, which stated, in part:

> 7. NATO personnel shall be immune from any form of arrest, investigation, or detention by the authorities in the FRY...
> 8. NATO personnel shall enjoy, together with their vehicles, vessels, aircraft, and equipment, free and unrestricted passage and unimpeded access throughout the FRY including associated airspace and territorial waters ...
> 11. NATO is granted the use of airports, roads, rails, and ports without payment of fees, duties, dues, tolls, or charges occasioned by mere use.[18]

Such requirements were a clear infringement of Yugoslavia's national sovereignty, and it was the opinion of many that no government in the world would voluntarily have accepted what would have amounted to a NATO occupation of the whole of Yugoslavia. This was also the view of the British House of Commons Foreign Affairs Committee, which stated in its Report of 23/5/00,

> We conclude that, whatever the actual impact of the Military Annex of the Rambouillet proposals on the negotiations, NATO was guilty of a serious blunder in allowing a Status of Forces Agreement into the package which would never have been acceptable to the Yugoslav side, since it was a significant infringement of its sovereignty.[19]

Indeed, many observers went further, and considered that the text had been deliberately made unacceptable, in order to ensure that NATO bombing could go ahead. Henry Kissinger described it as 'a provocation, an excuse to start bombing'.[20] George Kenney, a former US State Department Desk Officer for Yugoslavia, backed this view up with an account of what he was told about senior State Department views on this: 'An unimpeachable source who regularly travels with Secretary of State Madeline Albright told this [writer] that ... a senior State Department official had bragged that the United States "deliberately set the bar higher than the Serbs could accept". The Serbs needed, according to the official, a little bombing to see reason.'[21] Strangely, Adam LeBor, in his supposedly 'authoritative' biography of Milosevic, does not even mention Annex B in his discussion of Rambouillet.[22] In any case, Rambouillet had little to do with negotiations and everything to do with an ultimatum: either Yugoslavia accepted the proposals or she would be bombed.

The air offensive against Yugoslavia began on the night of 24 March 1999 although it was clear that the operation was not lawful under international law, since the UN charter prohibits the use of force except in self-defence. Article 2 of the UN charter states that 'all members shall refrain in their international relations from the threat or use of force against the territorial integrity or political independence of any state', and Article 53 specifically provides that the UN Security Council must authorize action: 'no enforcement action shall be taken under regional arrangements or by regional agencies without the authorisation of the Security Council'.

In the case of Yugoslavia this was clearly not a question of self-defence for NATO, and the bombardment did not take place under the authority of the Security Council, since two of the permanent members, Russia and China, were opposed to the attacks. The US, knowing it would be unable to get the action through the UN, circumvented that body, taking action through NATO on the spurious grounds that it was acting according to humanitarian principles. On 25 March 1999 the British Secretary of State for Foreign and Commonwealth Affairs announced that: 'We are acting on the legal principle that the action is justified to halt a humanitarian disaster.'[23] However, as Alice Mahon MP pointed out: 'Neither the British nor American governments, or NATO itself have ever produced any evidence for this [legal principle]. I know of no principle, in written law or in custom and practice.'[24] In fact, in

1986 the British Foreign Office had published an opinion stating, 'the overwhelming majority of contemporary legal opinion comes down against the existence of a right of humanitarian intervention'.[25] The British House of Commons Foreign Affairs Committee also commented on the issue of the legality of the bombing and the question of 'humanitarian intervention':

> 18. Our conclusion is that *Operation Allied Force* was contrary to the specific terms of what might be termed the basic law of the international community – the UN Charter ...
> 19. We conclude that, at the very least, the doctrine of humanitarian intervention has a tenuous basis in current international customary law, and that this renders NATO action legally questionable.

However, the FAC then went on to recommend that the Government should examine 'whether any new legal instrument is necessary to allow NATO to take action in future in the same manner as it did in Kosovo'. The FAC concluded that: 'NATO's military action, if of dubious legality in the current state of international law, was justified on moral grounds.'

This argument, that the military action was justified on moral grounds in order to protect the Kosovan Albanians from abuse, was taken up by Mark Littman QC, who observed that, while NATO force was used exclusively against the Serbs, contemporary official reports showed that Kosovan Albanians were probably more to blame for the hostilities at that time than the Serbs were. In fact, the UN Secretary General's report covering the period January to mid-March 1999

> showed that the resumption and continuation of hostilities in this period was initiated by the KLA and not by the Serbs. Thus the report accepted the statement of the OSCE that 'the current security environment in Kosovo is characterized by the disproportionate use of force, including mortar and tank fire, by the Yugoslav authorities in response to persistent attacks and provocations by the Kosovo Albanian paramilitaries'.[26]

Indeed, Littman also observes that the displacement of the Serb population in Kosovo at this time was proportionately as great as the displacement of the Kosovan Albanian population.

It is also worth noting that the Rambouillet text included the statement that: '"The economy of Kosovo shall function in accordance with free market principles." There was to be no restriction on the movement of "goods, services, and capital to Kosovo".'[27] This included the sale of Yugoslav federal property within Kosovo, such as the Trepca mining complex, which the *New York Times* described as 'war's glittering prize ... the most valuable piece of real estate in the Balkans ... worth at least $5billion'.[28]

THE NATO BOMBARDMENT

It seems likely that the NATO leadership expected Yugoslavia to capitulate after just a few days of bombing, but in fact the bombardment continued for 79 days, from 24 March to 10 June 1999. During this period, NATO made 37,000 bombing sorties. It is notable that, although the bombardment was under the auspices of NATO, it was overwhelmingly a US effort. As Peter Gowan has pointed out: 'The US flew over 80 per cent of the strike sorties, over 90 per cent of the electronic warfare missions, fired over 80 per cent of the guided air weapons and launched over 95 per cent of the Cruise missiles.'[29] Gowan also notes that command structures and decision-making were in US hands, so that, while US European NATO allies had a great symbolic importance in the conflict, the overwhelming US control had considerable political significance within Europe.

NATO estimates made during the bombardment were wildly exaggerated in a number of categories, presumably for public relations purposes. 5,000 members of the Yugoslav forces were reported killed and hundreds of tanks and heavy guns destroyed; 100,000 Albanian men were reported missing, supposedly killed by the Serbs. However, after the bombardment ended the reality emerged:

> in Kosovo NATO's bombing had destroyed 13 tanks and killed about 400 Serbian soldiers (an equal number had been killed by the Kosovo Liberation Army), and throughout Yugoslavia anywhere between 500 and 1,400 civilians had been killed by NATO bombs – a 'collateral damage' that could be three times higher than the Serbian military casualties.[30]

In fact, Yugoslav government estimates range from 1,200 to 5,700 civilians that may have been killed. Half a million Kosovan Albanians that were supposedly internally displaced turned out not to have been, and of the 800,000 who had sought refuge in neighbouring countries, the UNHCR estimated at the end of August that 765,000 had already returned to Kosovo. A more lasting factor, however, was that half of the Kosovan Serb population – approximately 100,000 – left Kosovo, or were driven out. Despite the assertions by allied leaders that Yugoslav forces were conducting 'genocide' against the Kosovan Albanians,[31] reports of mass killings and atrocities, such as the supposed hiding of the bodies of 700 murdered Kosovan Albanians in the Trepca mines, were often subsequently admitted to be incorrect. Investigative teams never found evidence of the large numbers of dead or missing, which NATO claimed. In the case of the Trepca mines accusation, it was the International Criminal Tribunal for the Former Yugoslavia which confirmed that the mines contained no bodies whatsoever.

There were a number of high profile blunders by the NATO forces, including: the striking of a passenger train in Serbia, killing 20 civilians; the bombing of a convoy of Kosovan Albanian refugees, killing 73 civilians; the bombing of the Chinese Embassy in Belgrade, killing three Chinese citizens; the bombing of the Belgrade television station; the bombing of a hospital and of a prison. It was also reported in April 1999 that NATO forces were using depleted uranium weapons, linked with cancers and birth defects in Iraq, and with Gulf War Syndrome, 'thought to be responsible for the deaths of more than 400 UK war veterans'.[32] US jets launched 31,000 depleted uranium warheads and shells during the bombing of Yugoslavia – and around 10,000 in Bosnia – in spite of the fact that the UN Human Rights Commission had condemned the use of radioactive projectiles. Madeline Albright insisted that there was absolutely no proof that there was a connection between depleted uranium and health problems, but this position was challenged by other concerned parties. It was subsequently queried by several NATO ambassadors as to why 'if the threat was so slight, did NATO military commanders send a warning before the peacekeeping mission in July 1999 citing a "possible toxic threat" and urging member states to take their own "preventive measures" in dealing with contamination risks'.[33] Indeed, a UN team that visited Bosnia and Kosovo found low-level radiation at 8 of the 11 sites sampled. Team chairman Pekka Haavisto recommended the fencing off of contaminated areas, expressing concern about the spread of radioactive materials: 'People had collected radioactive shards as souvenirs, and there were cows grazing in contaminated areas, which means the contaminated stuff can get into milk.'[34] Despite US assurances of the safety of depleted uranium weaponry, however, the EU ordered a formal inquiry into the health risks, following a number of cancer deaths of soldiers who had recently returned from the Balkans.

NATO planes also targeted the economic and social infrastructure of Serbia. As the Yugoslav Red Cross reported:

> The vital facilities of the Yugoslav economy have been destroyed. Destruction of factories, business and manufacturing plants amounted to over 100 billion USD. The destruction of the petrochemical industry, as well as the biggest artificial fertilizer factory has caused inestimable damage to agriculture and the life of the whole Yugoslav community, and it will be impossible to repair these consequences for years. The NATO bombing of the Yugoslav road and railway networks has destroyed and made inoperable over 50 bridges, all airports, numerous railway and bus stations.[35]

Houses, schools, hospitals, community and other institutions were also destroyed. None of these targets were focusing on Milosevic and Yugoslav military forces and they underline the longer-term economic interests of the US in Yugoslavia. As Diana Johnstone notes, quoting an unnamed German official, '"no nongovernmental humanitarian agency has the kind of money that will be needed to rebuild bridges or even dredge the wrecks out of the Danube". This was expected to provide "major leverage for western countries".'[36]

Cluster bombs were also used in the bombardment, although they are considered by many experts to be illegal as they have the effect of turning into landmines, if unexploded on initial impact. Indeed, the Foreign Affairs Committee observed:

> We recommend that the British Government consider carefully the experience of the use of cluster bombs in the Kosovo campaign to determine in future conflicts whether they are weapons which

pose so great a risk to civilians that they fall foul of the 1977
Protocol and should not be used in areas where civilians live.[37]

In addition to the impact of the bombing within Yugoslavia, there
was also a significant knock-on effect for Albania and Macedonia,
the two neighbouring countries who faced a huge influx of refugees
from the bombing. Both of these countries were extremely poor,
and the Macedonian government had grave concerns that the
refugee crisis would destabilize the delicate balance that existed
with the large Albanian minority within Macedonia itself.

On 9 June the NATO and Yugoslav military leaderships agreed
to the withdrawal of all Yugoslav forces from Kosovo and the entry
of an international security force.

The bombardment was concluded on 10 June with the adoption
of UN Resolution 1244, which formalized the arrangements. On 12
June Russian vehicles from Bosnia entered Kosovo and occupied
Pristina airport. NATO's KFOR troops entered Kosovo three hours
later. On 16 June Russian participation in KFOR was agreed
including the presence of Russian troops at Pristina airport. By 20
June Yugoslav forces had completed their withdrawal from Kosovo.

Given the figures for military casualties and destruction of
Yugoslav weaponry, the NATO bombing campaign could hardly be
said to have been a military defeat for Yugoslavia. The vast majority
of the Yugoslav population was also strongly anti-NATO and during
the bombing the population was very much united and support for
Milosevic increased. The bravery of the ordinary Yugoslavs,
defending their bridges and their factories, wearing target symbols
as human shields to ward off the bombing, touched people
throughout the world. What then led to the agreement of the
Yugoslav government to a peace settlement? In addition to the
obvious suffering inflicted upon the population and the damage
to the country's economy, there were two key factors. First, the
threat of a ground invasion, which was first implied by President
Clinton on 18 May, and then reinforced when five NATO defence
ministers considered the possibility on 27 May. Second, NATO
accepted that the Russians had a key role to play in bringing about
a diplomatic solution. In fact, ultimately, when the Serbian
parliament agreed on 3 June to a peace plan, it was proposed by
Viktor Chernomyrdin, who was President Yeltsin's special envoy

and Martii Ahtisaari, the Finnish President who represented the European Union.

NATO was facing problems of its own within the alliance, and coming under increasing pressure over the civilian casualties resulting from the bombardment. In effect, it had to step up the war, or back off, which it could not afford to do without terminally damaging the credibility of the alliance. The US did not want to deploy ground troops in Yugoslavia and so became slightly more flexible regarding the terms of a peace plan – for example, agreeing to the occupation of Kosovo taking place under the auspices of the UN, with Russian participation. The key to the problem for the US was Russia: if Chernomyrdin could convince Milosevic that no help was forthcoming from Russia and that he might as well give in, a peace settlement could be secured. As Daalder and O'Hanlon observe: 'By late May, Chernomyrdin was also telling Milosevic that in his estimation NATO would escalate to a ground war if necessary – and that Russia could not and would not do anything to prevent such an eventuality.'[38] This blow from Russia, the population of which was almost entirely in support of Yugoslavia, was no doubt what convinced the Yugoslav authorities to agree a settlement. It is notable, however, that even after the bombing, Yugoslavia did not have to accept a number of aspects of the Rambouillet text. Appendix B was not on the agenda at all, and the proposal for a referendum in the future of Kosovo – which Yugoslavia had initially been prepared to accept – was also excluded from the Agreement. Notwithstanding the UN/NATO protectorate that was to be established in Kosovo, the formal territorial integrity of Yugoslavia was no longer under threat. As Carl Jacobsen has observed: 'The "victory" declared by NATO ... constituted acceptance of the compromise Milosevic offered before the war.'[39]

KOSOVO AFTER THE WAR

On conclusion of the NATO bombardment, Kosovo became a UN protectorate, while still formally under Yugoslav sovereignty. It was run by three bodies: the UN Mission in Kososvo (UNMIK) was responsible for administration; the OSCE was responsible for law-making, organizing elections, and facilitating an independent media; and the KFOR military mission was in charge of security. The KLA was transformed into the Kosovan Protection Corps by the

UN, but in spite of Hashim Thaci declaring himself head of the provisional government, it rapidly became apparent that the Kosovan Albanian population actually preferred Rugova's LDK. On 18 October 1999 the *International Herald Tribune* reported on western opinion poll findings:

> The political party founded by Hashim Thaci ... would be crushed in provincial elections at all levels ... An opinion poll commissioned by a western organisation found Mr Rugova favored over Mr Thaci by a 4:1 margin ... A recent and less vigorous survey of 2,500 voters by an independent media organisation found that Mr Rugova would receive 92 percent of the vote in a two way race with Mr Thaci. And the rebels' support in former KLA strongholds, such as the Drenica area in central Kosovo, Mr Thaci's home base, has withered to single digits.[40]

When elections were eventually held, over two years later in November 2001, the margins were not so extreme, but they were still a convincing victory for Rugova: the LDK received more than 46 per cent of the vote, compared to the Democratic Party of Kosovo – the party of the KLA led by Hashim Thaci – which received 25.5 per cent of the vote. A coalition of parties representing the Serbian minority polled just under 11 per cent.

The position of the ethnic minorities in Kosovo remained a matter of grave concern, however, particularly for Serbs, Muslim slavs and Roma. As UNHCR/OSCE reported: 'The overall situation of ethnic minorities remains precarious ... Kosovo continues to be volatile and potentially dangerous, with ethnicity often remaining a determining factor in the risk of falling victim to crime.'[41] Fatal attacks, as well as 'numerous and regular' non-fatal attacks, and 'incidents of harassment and intimidation of varying degrees reported daily',[42] dogged the lives of the minority communities. Various mechanisms were put in place by KFOR for their protection, such as a permanent KFOR presence in minority areas, but even by March 2001, the British House of Commons Foreign Affairs Committee reported that: 'the Serbs remain bottled up in heavily defended enclaves. There are frequent incidents of intimidation and violence, as well as attacks on Serb religious sites.'[43]

It is also notable that large numbers of Kosovan Serbs and other minority communities have departed from the province. As the International Committee of the Red Cross pointed out in 2000:

'Some 40,000 KFOR troops are present, complemented by a UN international police force in charge of enforcing law and order. Despite this massive international presence, the Serb community and other minorities are being expelled. More than 200,000 have already left, mostly for Serbia and Montenegro.'[44] For example, in 1998 UNHCR estimated that 20,000 Serbs lived in Pristina; by early 2000, the UNHCR estimated the number at around 700 to 800.[45] Peter Gowan describes this as the result of the KLA leadership taking 'radical measures to consolidate their grip on the whole of Kosovo's population, pursuing a covert but very effective campaign of ethnic terror and ethnic cleansing against Serbs, Roma and other non-Albanian ethnic groups within Kosovo'.[46] Problems have also occurred within the policing of the province, and some members of the police service have been dismissed for unacceptable behaviour, including victimization of minorities. As the UNHCR/OSCE Report observes: 'An important aspect linked to the question of policing is that of widespread reports that former members of the KLA and/or provisional members of the Kosovo Protection Corps ... or persons claiming to be such, continue to be engaged in irregular and illegal policing activities.'[47]

9
Bringing down Milosevic and what came after

In September 2000, Milosevic was defeated in the Yugoslav presidential election by Vojislav Kostunica. The US and the EU used these elections finally to achieve what they had been trying to do for over a decade, and had failed to do through bombing – to satisfy their own economic and strategic goals in the post-Soviet period. These included the integration of all of the component republics of the former Yugoslavia into the free-market economic system, and the removal of a government in Belgrade which had not only a socialist economic orientation, but also a strategic orientation away from NATO and towards Russia. The removal of Milosevic was essential to this goal, since he continued to defend the socialized features of the economy, and his removal did indeed end the pursuit by Yugoslavia of economic and strategic self-determination. The presidency of Kostunica as the acceptable face of Yugoslav patriotism was the final stage in the achievement of post-Soviet western goals in Yugoslavia.

Kostunica was deeply critical of NATO and the bombing – otherwise he would never have been elected – but he was receptive to western financial institutions and neo-liberal economic reform and so was able to bring about the economic system change that the west so greatly desired. To portray the elections as a domestic, democratic victory over dictatorship is misleading and inaccurate. First, as explained below, Milosevic was not a dictator, and second, the elections were subject to considerable external intervention – military, economic and political – rendering them far from fair and democratic. Massive funding, training and advice were provided to promote the opposition forces and secure their eventual success.

Following Milosevic's defeat, an uneasy partnership existed in the leadership of the country between President Kostunica on the one hand, and Prime Minister Djindjic on the other. Djindjic, the most pro-western of the former opposition politicians – in effect a Trojan Horse for the IMF – was responsible for handing Milosevic over to the war crimes tribunal at the Hague – which Kostunica opposed, arguing that he should be tried in Yugoslavia. Djindjic also favoured the transformation of Yugoslavia into the Union of Serbia and Montenegro, whereas Kostunica initially opposed this move. The restructuring of the Yugoslav economy proceeded under their leadership prior to the assassination of Djindjic in March 2003.

The corollary of the western promotion of the KLA in Kosovo was played out in the neighbouring republic of Macedonia, which also had a large ethnic Albanian minority. KLA-linked organizations began to destabilize the regions closest to Kosovo, leading to fears that attempts were being made to revive the Greater Albanian vision. Widespread violence has so far been avoided.

The future direction of Montenegro – the other republic within the Federal Republic of Yugoslavia – was also uncertain. President Milo Djukanovic of Montenegro strongly sought independence from the Federation. He had been supported in this aim by the west prior to the departure of Milosevic, but subsequently he was encouraged – in particular by the EU – to remain within the Federation, with the goal of a looser union.

Moves by Javier Solana on behalf of the EU in early 2002, to push for the final end of Yugoslavia, bore fruit on 31 May 2002. The Yugoslav parliament voted – by 23 votes to 6 in the upper house, and 74 to 23 in the lower house – to abolish the Yugoslav federation and replace it with a looser Union of Serbia and Montenegro. The parliaments of Serbia and Montenegro had already accepted the plan. As Serbian deputy prime minister Zarko Korac observed: 'Many people will see this as the day that Yugoslavia died, because the name is no longer mentioned in the agreement – the new state is called Serbia and Montenegro.'[1] The union provides for a joint parliamentary chamber as well as separate Serb and Montenegrin ones. Banking and customs systems will remain separate but there will be a joint army and a shared seat with alternating occupancy at the United Nations and other international institutions. The new state formally came into existence in February 2003.

POLITICS IN SERBIA

As Robert Thomas observes, Milosevic and the Serbian Socialist Party (SPS) were politically hegemonic from 1990–98.[2] Serbia under

Milosevic was not, as he points out, 'a dictatorship in the *totalitarian* sense of the word. Opposition political parties, and civic organizations, continued to operate throughout this period, and the independent media continued to publish and broadcast.'[3] Thomas does, however, criticize the SPS for remaining highly interlinked with the state rather than functioning as a pluralist political party – describing it as a 'state-dependent agency'. While this may be the case, it is also quite clear that Milosevic and the SPS had genuine political support demonstrated through the ballot box, and thus the description of the Milosevic leadership as a dictatorship is not accurate and stems from factors other than any major deficit in political democracy. Thomas can perhaps help to explain this matter. He has also observed that Milosevic's leadership had bypassed 'the processes of "transition" that were taking root in other countries of Central and Eastern Europe', and suggests that a fully democratic and pluralist polity requires not only a functioning political democracy, but also dispersal of economic power.[4] This is the nub of the matter – that Milosevic was not undertaking full free-market economic reform and remained committed to some elements of a socialist economy. This was reflected in the high degree of loyalty he continued to enjoy amongst some sections of the electorate, for: 'Milosevic's support remained strongest among the rural population and industrial workers of Serbia.'[5]

The pattern of electoral choice during the 1990s also reflects quite clearly the nature of the political situation at that time – rather than any manipulation or distortion of political opinion or results. In the first parliamentary election in Serbia in 1990 the SPS took 46.4 per cent of the vote, Vuk Draskovic's Serbian Renewal Party (anti-communist nationalist) 15.8 per cent, and Zoran Djindjic's Democratic Party (pro-western) 7.4 per cent. These parties played a role throughout the 1990s in shifting combinations and alliances, according to their political positions and the views of the voters. In the mid-1990s the strongly nationalist Serbian Radical Party (SRS), led by Vojislav Seselj, began to make a greater impact upon the political scene, mobilizing popular anger against the Dayton Accords and winning the support of dissatisfied electors from both the SPS and the other opposition forces. In the parliamentary election of 1997, the SRS had a strong showing, beating Draskovic's Serbian Renewal Movement into a poor third place, and entering a coalition government with the SPS, which did not have enough seats to govern alone. In 1999 Draskovic briefly joined Milosevic's administration. The results may not have been to western tastes, but they were clearly the choice of the Serbian electorate.

This pattern in Serbian politics was somewhat borne out by the analysis in 1996, of Zoran Djindjic, who later became the pro-western prime minister of Serbia, after the defeat of Milosevic in 2000. He analysed the trends in Serbian politics, noting that there were basically three political positions: the socialist position, the radical national populist tradition, and the position as he describes it, 'of development and modernisation', or the pro-western position.[6] The politicians that he associated with these positions were respectively Milosevic, Seselj and at times Draskovic, and Djindjic himself. The goal which Djindjic sought – to build a united, pro-western opposition to Milosevic – was a difficult one to achieve, since elements of the national populist opposition had often informally supported Milosevic in defence of the national interest in the early 1990s, and the west was seen by many as the enemy of the Serbs, particularly after Dayton. The SPS was the largest single party but did not always have enough support to govern alone. The opposition parties were numerous but usually small and, in order to mount an effective challenge to the SPS, they had to unite. Thus, it was necessary for all parties to build coalitions and alliances.

On the left the SPS's main partner from the mid-1990s emerged as the Yugoslav United Left (JUL), previously the JNA-originated League of Communists – Movement for Yugoslavia, relaunched in March 1995. The JUL as Adam LeBor points out, was 'an alliance of twenty-one parties, mostly leftist or "Yugo-nostalgic"'.[7] LeBor notes two strands within JUL – red businessmen like the secretary general Zoran Todorovic, and intellectuals such as Ljubisa Ristic, the avant-garde theatre director, who had worked at the Riverside Studios in London. 'Such figures saw JUL as a guarantor of the old Yugoslavia's multi-ethnic, and anti-imperialist, heritage. The party was strongly anti-nationalist, and virulently attacked Radovan Karadzic.'[8] Milosevic's wife, Mirjana Markovic was a leading figure in JUL. From 1995 Milosevic appeared to attempt to consolidate the left within Serbia, moving away from the more nationalist framework that had prevailed during the wars in Croatia and Bosnia: in November, six leading figures in the SPS, known as the 'nationalist' faction, were removed from office. Closer links were established politically and economically with China, to the extent that: 'Belgrade wits dubbed

JUL "The Communist Party of China in Serbia".[9] The success of the Chinese economic reforms, which combined a framework of state ownership and planning with extensive opportunities for foreign investment and market developments, were of interest to Milosevic, who was still committed to a socialist economic framework. The relative success of Chinese-style economic reforms in Cuba and Vietnam may have convinced him that they could contain elements that were also appropriate for Yugoslavia.

The opposition to the SPS also sought to consolidate its position. In 1996, Djindjic's Democratic Party, Draskovic's Serbian Renewal Movement and Vesna Pesic's liberal Civic Alliance joined together to form the coalition Zajedno ('Together'). Zajedno also worked on occasions with the Democratic Party of Serbia, under the leadership of Vojislav Kostunica, later to be President of Yugoslavia after defeating Milosevic in 2000. Zajedno's first opportunity at the polls was in November 1996 when federal and local elections took place. In the federal elections the SPS-led coalition with JUL and the New Democracy Party took 64 seats, Zajedno 22, and the strongly nationalist Serbian Radical Party 16. The Radical vote was to some extent an indication of dissatisfaction by those who felt that Milosevic had compromised too much at Dayton and had failed to defend the Bosnian Serbs. Indeed, it should be noted that the opposition was a complex and diverse political animal, and not primarily a pro-western liberal force that thought Milosevic was a rabid nationalist. As Robert Thomas quotes, commenting on the nature of an opposition protest: 'In the middle of a speech about the values of the democratic, civic state and its integration into Europe the crowd spontaneously began to chant the inappropriate slogan "Fuck you, Slobo, you betrayed the Krajina".'[10]

In the local elections, Zajedno performed better, winning in more than a dozen cities and towns where the SPS was weaker and the urban populations more orientated towards pro-western ideas, such as Belgrade, Nis, and Novi Sad. However, Milosevic was not prepared to allow the opposition to take up its places in the town halls: he could see the looming, incremental breakdown of the system. The election results were annulled and a third round of voting was called, which Zajedno boycotted. After weeks of widespread – and occasionally violent – street protests, Milosevic, under pressure from the OSCE, backed down, and in February 1997 the Zajedno victories were recognized, with Zoran Djindjic becoming Mayor of

Belgrade. For a time Zajedno was courted by senior figures in western governments and began to outline and develop a programme of reform, including accession to the EU by 2005. However, by mid-1997, relations between the parties within Zajedno had broken down, largely over distribution of future offices.

In the light of these developments, the SPS began during 1997 to re-emphasize the importance of patriotic unity, both seeing the Zajedno advances as the thin end of the wedge – on the way to losing the country to western interests, and also concerned about the growing support for the SRS. As a spokesperson for the Belgrade SPS stated:

> In our conditions today linked and complex left-wing and democratic forces have the primary objective of preserving the state and reconstructing the country. Their primary role thus has an explicitly patriotic character. So in our current circumstances the alliance of left-wing and democratic forces is, above all, an alliance of patriotic forces. To this end it should thoroughly mobilise society towards the notions of unity and the country's reconstruction.[11]

This indicated a readiness to work with the nationalists, if necessary, to defeat the western-oriented liberals, who would ultimately bring about a full break with the socialist system by embracing neo-liberal economics.

The Serbian parliamentary elections of September 1997 were boycotted by Djindjic's Democratic Party (DS), which led to conflict between the supporters of DS and their former Zajedno partners, Draskovic's Serbian Renewal Movement (SPO). The results gave 110 seats to the left coalition, 45 seats to SPO and 82 seats to the Serbian Radical Party (SRS). Negotiations began between the SPS and SPO over the composition of a coalition government. This now threw the opposition into disarray, because not only was Draskovic preparing to work with Milosevic, but the DS and other parties that had boycotted the elections, such as Kostunica's Democratic Party of Serbia and the Civic Alliance, had now become extra-parliamentary parties. Negotiations with the SPO were still going on in March 1998, when the crisis in Kosovo began to come to a head. Draskovic refused to take part in a Serbian government delegation to Pristina to meet Albanian political leaders, and shortly thereafter negotiations began between the SPS and the SRS, as a matter of urgency, to form a coalition government. The crisis in Kosovo necessitated a functioning and effective government. An agreement was reached on 24 March, and a new government was announced, with ministerial positions comprising 15 SPS, 5 JUL and 15 SRS. The new government made a Declaration of National Unity and almost immediately held a referendum on the question: 'Will you accept the participation of foreign representatives in resolving the Kosovo problem?' The result was a 95 per cent rejection of foreign participation, on a 73 per cent turnout.

THE PRESIDENTIAL ELECTION OF 2000

The NATO bombardment of Yugoslavia unified the country behind the government and Milosevic articulated the views of virtually all Serbs in defence of their national sovereignty. When the war concluded in June 1999, however, with Milosevic still in power, the political opposition became the recipient of considerable western attention. It was funded and encouraged to unify in order to present an effective challenge to the SPS and Milosevic and, as Jonathan Eyal has observed, 'to achieve through the ballot box what NATO's bombing campaign failed to accomplish: the removal of Mr Milosevic'.[12] In the summer of 2000 Milosevic announced that he was going to stand for re-election as President of Yugoslavia before his term was up, and that he was going to change the method of election to a direct vote by the electorate, rather than by the parliament. According to Diana Johnstone, his advisers had led him to believe that he was ahead in the opinion polls and would gain the necessary 50 per cent to win in the first round.[13] Eighteen opposition parties joined together to form the Democratic opposition of Serbia, and field a common candidate, Vojislav Kostunica, at that time a 56-year-old constitutional lawyer. Kostunica was a credible candidate – moderate Serbian nationalist, anti-NATO – which was essential for any candidate to be successful – but amenable to full-scale economic reform. The participation of the US in the choice of opposition candidate and the conduct of his campaign, is well known. As the *International Herald Tribune* reported in October 1999, 20 opposition leaders attended a seminar in Budapest, organized by the Washington-based National Democratic Institute, to discuss the results of an opinion poll conducted by a US company in Serbia. The poll showed that Milosevic had an unfavourable rating of around 70 per cent with voters, but that Djindjic and Draskovic were almost as unpopular. Kostunica, on the other hand, had an unfavourable rating of only 29 per cent, and a favourable rating of 49 per cent. 'Part of Mr Kostunica's appeal, the polls showed, was that he was widely perceived as anti-American. Because he was an outspoken critic of the NATO bombing of Serbia, it was difficult for the Milosevic government to label him as a western stooge or a traitor to Serbian interests.'[14]

The *IHT* described the seminar in Budapest as the start of 'an extraordinary U.S. effort to unseat a foreign head of state'. Over the following year

> U.S.-funded consultants played a crucial role in virtually every facet of the anti-Milosevic drive, running tracking polls, training thousands of opposition activists and helping to organize a vitally important parallel vote count. U.S. taxpayers paid for 5,000 cans of spray paint used by student activists to scrawl anti-Milosevic graffiti on walls across Serbia and 2.5 million stickers with the slogan 'He's Finished,' which became the revolution's catchphrase.[15]

US advisers impressed upon the opposition that their success depended upon them remaining united and they managed to achieve this goal. The key to the process was, of course, money, and plenty of this was forthcoming from both the US and EU. The US 'democracy-building effort' was funded by congressional appropriations of around $10 million in fiscal 1999, and $31 million in 2000. The day after the election took place, the US House of Representatives voted a further $105 million. The lead role in channelling the funding prior to the election was taken by the State Department and the US Agency for International Development, via commercial contractors, the National Democratic Institute and the International Republican Institute. Both major US parties lent their support to opposition forces – the Democrats working with the political parties, and the Republicans backing the student movement Otpor. Indeed, in March 2000, the Republican institute paid for 24 Otpor leaders 'to attend a seminar on non-violent resistance at the Hilton Hotel in Budapest', where they learnt about organizing strikes, overcoming fear and how to undermine a dictatorial regime.[16]

Other methods were also employed to affect the electoral process. US and EU sanctions were creating a desperate economic situation and it was made quite clear that sanctions would not be lifted unless Milosevic was ousted. Before the election was complete, the EU issued a statement saying that any claim by Milosevic to be the victor would be fraudulent. On election day itself, US and Croatian forces held joint military exercises off the coast of Montenegro and 15 British warships were moved into the Mediterranean. It is also interesting to note that a survey of radio listening habits, conducted by Belgrade University in October 2000, showed that the US's Radio Free Europe/Radio Liberty 'was the most listened-to broadcaster since August 1999 and especially during the political crisis in the fall of 2000 ... During the days between 24 September and 3 October, RFE/RL's listenership rating was 37 percent or nearly double that of the BBC (19 percent) and more than state-run Radio Belgrade's 31 percent.'[17]

The first round of the elections took place on 24 September. The constitution requires the winner to achieve 50 per cent of the vote in the first round, otherwise a second round is required. The election commission declared that Kostunica had achieved 48 per cent of the vote, and Milosevic 38 per cent of the vote, with Mihailovic of the Serbian Renewal Movement coming a poor fourth. The opposition, however, declared that fraud had occurred and that Kostunica was the outright winner, refusing to countenance a second round, in spite of the fact that over 200 observers from 54 countries had stated that the election was fair, and that opposition representatives on the polling station committees had also agreed the results. This was presumably because in a second round it was conceivable that those who had supported Mihailovic and others in the first round might transfer their support to Milosevic and ensure his election. The two chamber federal assembly was also elected, where the left won a majority as a result of an opposition boycott in Montenegro. A 5-day campaign of civil disobedience, including strikes and school boycotts, was initiated by the opposition. A few days before the second round was due to take place on 8 October, the Constitutional Court annulled the elections, declaring that Milosevic would finish his term of office and that new presidential elections would be held the following summer. This announcement appeared to provoke a spontaneous outburst culminating in violent protest in Belgrade. The parliament was stormed, the television station set on fire and the SPS and JUL headquarters were ransacked. During these events, the army remained in barracks, leading to the assumption that its leaders had come to an agreement with the opposition. Eventually, Kostunica was declared president and Milosevic accepted defeat, stating that he would remain active in politics. The first foreign leader to visit Yugoslavia after the election was Russian Foreign Minister Ivanov, who met both Kostunica and Milosevic and presumably persuaded Milosevic to accept defeat gracefully.

There was a very rapid acceptance by state forces of the new situation. The federal Prime Minister Momir Bulatovic, who was a key Milosevic ally, resigned with all his cabinet, as did the Serbian Interior Minister Vlajko Stojilkovic. The new leadership commenced the rapid removal of state media leaders, managers, university heads and so on, and there were calls for a purge of Milosevic supporters in education. In the Serbian parliamentary elections of December that year the SPS was defeated, and Djindjic became prime minister of Serbia. It was clear that this was not just a question of one man being replaced – this was the finalization of a system change. The political leadership of Yugoslavia had now definitively changed: the new leaders rejected Milosevic's commitment to elements of a socialized economy – notably the maintenance of a large state sector – and now economic reform could be pushed through. Once economic reform had been achieved, the SPS would cease to be a threat to western interests, even if it remained a popular party that might participate in future governments. Milosevic's attempts to retain power in Yugoslavia seem more likely to have been motivated by the desire to maintain the hybrid form of socialist economy and class politics that existed in Yugoslavia, than to cling to power to satisfy his own personal ambitions. Once the Soviet Union had collapsed, together with the demise of socialism in eastern Europe, and the economic and strategic integration of the former socialist countries had begun, however, Milosevic's desire was unrealizable. A similar situation faced the former communist parties in both Bulgaria and Romania in the early years after 1989. Both were elected to govern their countries, with considerable popular support, and were committed to the maintenance of aspects of the socialist economic system. Following the demise of the Soviet Union at the end of 1991, the possibility of an alternative economic and political pole was removed, and both were eventually pressurized by the western institutions to introduce neo-liberal economic reforms. These resulted in considerable economic hardship for the populations, and the parties' popular support was, at least temporarily, greatly reduced.

The likely economic orientation of the new government was clearly outlined by Mladjan Dinkic, the chief economist of the opposition, as early as 26 September, when he commented, 'we are thinking of adopting ... a shock therapy in some areas, and mild and gradual reforms in others'.[18] He confirmed that the country's reserves had not been plundered by leading officials, as had been alleged for years: 'The foreign currency and gold reserves seem to be at a satisfactory level of about DM385 million, which indicates that nobody in the power structure dared take them out of the country.'[19] Dinkic also stated that Dragoslav Avramovic, former governor of the National Bank, had drafted a letter of intent, requesting read-mission to the IMF and World Bank, and including a memorandum on Economic and Financial Policies. Yugoslavia had lost its seats on these bodies when its membership of the UN was suspended in the early 1990s over the wars in Croatia and Bosnia.[20]

Shortly after the election, Dinkic travelled to Bulgaria to meet rep-resentatives of the IMF, World Bank and NATO at a donor conference. The requirements of the donors were anticipated to be: an end of government price controls; introduction of free markets and an end to protectionism; an end to social protection; a freeze on credit to business; cutbacks in workforces and wages; and privatization or liquidation of state or socially owned enter-prises. In other words, a continuation of the IMF policies which had wreaked so much havoc in the 1980s, and had devastated the economies of the other former socialist countries after 1989. Indeed, the ending of subsidies on certain goods meant that only a month after the presidential election, key prices had soared. For example, the price of oil in Belgrade had increased by over 300 per cent from 15 to 51 dinars, of bread by over 200 per cent from 6 to 14 dinars, and of sugar by over 700 per cent from 6 to 46 dinars. These increases were described by customers as 'democratic prices'.[21]

In early October 2000, the EU lifted the oil embargo and flight ban against Serbia, and cancelled all sanctions except those 'directed at Milosevic and all persons connected with him'.[22] The EU also observed that as the Serbian people had opted 'for democracy and Europe', that the EU would change its policy appropriately, immediately including Yugoslavia into the EU programme for aid to Balkan countries. They proposed the formation of a joint EU–Yugoslavia working group to reach agreement on stabilization and association, and said that, together with international financial institutions, they would 'examine conditions for the speediest possible integration of Yugoslavia into the international financial community'.[23]

Dinkic, who became governor of the National Bank, and the rest of his economic team, moved ahead with the anticipated privatization and restructuring. In early 2002, the four biggest state-owned banks had their licences removed after the Yugoslav National Bank decided against rescuing them from their debt problems. As Robert Wright commented in the *Financial Times*:

> It was the most dramatic move yet by the group of young mostly western-trained men in charge of Serbia's economic reforms under Zoran Djindjic, the prime minister ... Their aggressive approach contrasts sharply with the more gradualist approach of other former Yugoslav states such as Slovenia and Croatia. Those countries' troubled banks were nursed expensively back to health.[24]

The phasing-out of price controls, which once covered 70 per cent of goods, has continued, continuing to add to inflation and, according to Wright, there are already complaints that some household utility bills are higher than average salaries. In addition: 'Unemployment may also rise from an already high 870,000 – more than 25 per cent of the workforce – as companies are restructured, privatised or put into bankruptcy.'[25] Considerable hardship is being experienced by the Serbs as a result of the reform programme.

MACEDONIA AND MONTENEGRO

The Former Yugoslav Republic of Macedonia – officially so known because of Greek hostility to the use of the name Macedonia through fear of irredentism – faced serious problems in the years following the NATO bombardment of Kosovo. Macedonia has an ethnic Albanian minority population of around 20 per cent, concentrated largely in the regions adjoining Kosovo and Albania. Ethnic Albanian extremists – quite probably from the KLA and associated organizations – began to stir up secessionist demands and anti-Macedonian sentiment amongst them. In December 2000, the *International Herald Tribune* reported the dangers: 'according to western officials, there are worrying signs that arms are flowing from Kosovo to Macedonia, which has a large ethnic Albanian minority'.[26] While demands for the unity of ethnic Albanians in Macedonia with those in Kosovo had been heard within Yugoslavia since the 1960s, this was very much a minority perspective. It had never achieved the profile or support that the campaign of the Albanians in Kosovo did, and there was a peaceful relationship between the different communities. In fact, a major mistake was made in formulating the new constitution for Macedonia when it declared independence from Yugoslavia. The constitution was worded so that Macedonia was redefined as: 'the nation state of Macedonian people, in which full equality as citizens and permanent coexistence with the Macedonian people is provided for Albanians, Turks, Vlachs, Roma and other nationalities living in the Republic of Macedonia'. This replaced the previous formulation, which described Macedonia as 'the state of the Macedonian people and the Albanian and Turkish minorities'. Clearly there is a difference in emphasis within these statements and the new constitution can be seen as downgrading the constitutional status of non-ethnic Macedonians within the state. The most immediate reason for the tension, however, was the failure of KFOR properly to disband and disarm the KLA, and to prevent the KLA's ethnic cleansing of the Serbs and other minorities in Kosovo. Responsibility should also be laid at the door of the leading NATO countries, and in particular the US, for raising the status of the KLA to that of international actor at the Rambouillet talks and supporting it militarily. In effect, NATO had inflated a tiny terrorist group into a fully grown monster to serve its own ends – a pretext to attack Yugoslavia – and was now having difficulty trying to put the monster back in its cage. It is interesting to note the observation of Peter Finn from the *International Herald Tribune*, with regard to the stirring-up of tensions in Macedonia: 'So the longtime Serbian assertion that the danger in the Balkans was not a "Greater Serbia" but a "Greater Albania" is beginning to gain currency in Western circles where it was long dismissed as cant.'[27]

In December 2000 President Milo Djukanovic of Montenegro made his first visit to Belgrade for two years, to attend a meeting of Yugoslavia's Supreme Defence Council, chaired by the new president, Kostunica. Djukanovic broke with Milosevic in 1997 and subsequently pressed for independence for Montenegro with support from the west. A number of anti-Yugoslav steps had been taken, including abandoning the dinar and adopting the German mark as Montenegro's currency. With the change in Yugoslav leadership, the west moved away from support for Montenegrin independence, although Djukanovic continued to pursue the goal. Kostunica was eager to retain Montenegro within the federation. In early 2001 Djukanovic visited Washington to argue for independence, but Secretary of State Colin Powell refused to see him, a refusal based, according to administration officials, 'on a desire not to encourage the further changing of borders in the region'.[28] Montenegrin independence would, it was argued, also encourage other claims: for Kosovan independence, for unity of the Bosnian Serb entity with Serbia, for changes to the borders to Macedonia to accommodate ethnic Albanian demands, and so on. A real danger of the proposed independence was the threat to the internal stability of Montenegro itself, where the population is split over the prospect of independence. Even according to Djukanovic's supporters, only just over 50 per cent of the population back independence, so the possibility of conflict exists.[29]

In February 2002, under heavy pressure from the EU – including the threat of aid cuts – Djukanovic agreed to abandon the immediate goal of independence. The Federal Republic of Yugoslavia was replaced by the Union of Serbia and Montenegro on 4 February 2003.

10
Victors' justice?
The trial of Slobodan Milosevic

The decision in 2002 to terminate the Federal Republic of Yugoslavia and replace it with the Union of Serbia and Montenegro, and its realization in 2003, symbolized the final breaking of the south slav dream – the desire to achieve unity and self-determination for the south slav peoples. For part of the twentieth century this dream had been a reality – most fully realized during the Tito period. Two factors were crucial in this realization: first, that the interests of foreign powers did not predominate in determining the development of Yugoslavia; second, that the interests of each component nation was met within a united, federal Yugoslavia. In the post-war period Tito succeeded in achieving a balance in both respects. The balance was broken, however, due primarily to external factors, but also to related internal ones. The political and economic offensive of the US towards the socialist countries in the 1980s, facilitated by the weakness of the Soviet Union and the policies of Mikhail Gorbachev, led to crisis and destabilization within Yugoslavia as a result of IMF conditionality and reform. The promotion of secessionist tendencies within Yugoslavia and amongst Yugoslavs abroad – in particular by the German state – exacerbated the problems. Within Yugoslavia itself, Tito had negotiated an effective balance between the different constituent nations, based on political and economic devolution and power-sharing. This also began to break down in the 1980s under the pressure of the economic crisis and foreign encouragement of some of the political elements in some of the constituent republics – primarily secessionist, pro-free-market forces in Slovenia and Croatia. In fact, the origins of this tendency were located somewhat earlier in the development of Yugoslavia. Aspects of the self-management and devolution reforms as early as the 1960s began to allow the development of private enterprise to the extent that nascent capitalist economic interests emerged. In Croatia and Slovenia these were economically oriented towards Germany and Austria, and they sought greater political and economic self-determination and ultimately independence. Accordingly, they backed the re-Balkanization of the region and the break-up of Yugoslavia to achieve these ends, and were encouraged by a number of western powers to do so.

The creation of Yugoslavia, however, had resolved a number of problems that re-Balkanization could not. The ethnic complexity of the region meant that nationally homogeneous successor states could not just neatly emerge to replace the Yugoslav federation where all rights and equalities had been guaranteed under complex constitutional arrangements. The socialist character of the Yugoslav federation also meant that huge efforts were made to ensure the equal economic development of the constituent republics and the opportunities of all citizens. While fully even development was never achieved, there was considerable redistribution of the state's assets to support the development of economically weaker areas, and a viable economy, organized around the needs of the Yugoslav peoples, was achieved. In short, the vital questions of independence and self-determination – both economically and politically – for the south slav peoples were only effectively resolved in the socialist federation. With the fragmentation of the federation and the introduction of capitalism, came war and then recolonization. The latter occurred on an economic basis in all republics, and in some cases such as Bosnia and Kosovo, it also occurred institutionally.

While these issues were understood by many Yugoslavs in all the constituent republics – and there was much under-reported opposition to the break-up – it was in Serbia and amongst the Serbs living outside the Serbian republic, that these issues had most resonance. The Serbs were the largest constituent nation, and the right to self-determination of all Serbs – as of all of the nations of Yugoslavia – was guaranteed under the Yugoslav constitution, irrespective of the republic in which they resided. While the federation existed, their rights were ensured, but once Croatia and Bosnia declared independence, their right to self-determination was unconstitutionally withdrawn. They found themselves, without their consent, in the case of Croatia, living in a state in which they did not have full citizenship rights. The Serbs were not alone in understanding the implications of the break-up, for initially Bosnia, Macedonia and Montenegro also opposed the break-up because of the risks this posed of irredentism and inter-ethnic conflict.

Thus it was the Serbs – who had been the key nation in unifying Yugoslavia – who held out the longest for the maintenance and self-determination of that state. By the 1990s the politically flawed, but residually socialist Yugoslav leadership realized that self-determination relied upon economic sovereignty, which would be ended with the introduction of neo-liberal economic reform. Without external allies, and increasingly losing support internally – to a great extent due to the economic impact of sanctions on the living conditions of ordinary people – Milosevic on occasion attempted to suppress the opposition. The refusal to recognize Zajedno victories in the local elections was an example of this, but ultimately he accepted the logic of the international situation as it applied to his own country: a state with socialist economic features, attempting to operate outside the institutional framework set by the EU and NATO, would not be tolerated. Together the Serbs rejected this lesson during the NATO bombing of 1999, but by 2000 the trend could no longer be bucked, and Milosevic was removed from power. Soon afterwards, he was sent to the Hague to face charges relating to to the wars in Croatia, Bosnia and Kosovo. At the time of writing, the trial of Slobodan Milosevic before the International Criminal Tribunal for the former Yugoslavia still continues.

THE CHARGES

The trial, which opened in the Hague on 12 February 2002, has been described as 'Europe's most important war crimes case since Nazi leaders were tried at Nuremberg'.[1] Milosevic, the only head of state to be indicted while in office, is accused of 66 charges arising from the wars in Croatia between 1991 and 1992, Bosnia between 1992 and 1995 and Kosovo in 1999. In Croatia, he is accused of crimes against humanity and of being responsible for the murder of hundreds of civilians, and the expulsion of 170,000 non-Serbs from their homes, including atrocities committed in Vukovar. In Bosnia the accusations are of genocide, crimes against humanity and breaches of the Geneva Convention. He is charged with being responsible for the murder of thousands of Bosnians, including the massacre at Srebrenica in July 1995. In Kosovo, Milosevic and four others are accused of crimes against humanity in the period from January to June 1999, including the alleged massacre at Racak in January 1999, and violation of the laws or customs of war and the deportation of 800,000 Kosovan Albanians. The indictment also includes charges stemming from acts of sexual violence allegedly committed by Yugoslav soldiers, for which Milosevic – as army commander-in-chief – had direct responsibility.

As the trial commenced, chief UN prosecutor Carla del Ponte expressed confidence to the press that there was enough evidence to prove that Milosevic was guilty of the gravest crimes. In her opening statement she said that Milosevic had been motivated by a 'quest for power' and had inflicted 'medieval savagery and a calculated cruelty that went far beyond the bounds of legitimate warfare' in what deputy prosecutor Geoffrey Nice described as 'the joint criminal enterprise' to create a greater Serbia.

Other voices have, however, been heard – in addition to Milosevic's own – putting forward differing interpretations of events. An article in the *Los Angeles Times* stated: 'Milosevic, as a scapegoat in a show trial with a predestined outcome, would be a perfect medium to exorcise the guilt of those who are trying to obliterate their complicity in provoking the Balkan Wars.'[2] Milosevic describes the trial as 'an evil and hostile attack aimed at justifying the crimes committed against my country', and he has some considerable support for this viewpoint. Perhaps most notable is Ramsay Clark, a former US attorney-general, and there are a number of lawyers and celebrities internationally, like the playwright Harold Pinter, who have supported the International Committee to Defend Slobodan Milosevic. Given the highly-contested nature of the reasons for the break-up of Yugoslavia in the 1990s and the controversy over the illegal bombing of Yugoslavia in 1999, there is a strong body of international opinion which holds that Milosevic is on trial because he opposed the break-up of Yugoslavia and its integration into western free-market institutions, and that the Hague process is the application of 'victors' justice'. Indeed, the methods by which he was brought to the Hague have also been the target of much criticism, lending themselves to the view that he was 'sold' by Djindjic for financial support which has been noticeably unforthcoming.

Milosevic rejects the legitimacy of the court and has refused to appoint defence lawyers. He refused to enter a plea of guilty or not guilty and not-guilty was entered on his behalf by the court. Originally trained as a lawyer in Belgrade, Milosevic has been conducting his own case, cross-examining witnesses and exposing inconsistencies and inaccuracies, and he is considered by many, particularly within Serbia, to be making an impressive case. As Tim

Judah has observed: 'the trial has so far only served to reinforce the widespread Serbian prejudice that the tribunal is an anti-Serb kangaroo court and that Milosevic will emerge, as he has already declared, as the "moral victor"'.[3] The *Observer* newspaper has reported that the trial, televised live on Serbian television, is enormously popular. One poll showed that 41.6 per cent of Serbs give Milosevic five out of five for his performance at the trial.[4]

The first phase of the trial, which has focused on the charges related to Kosovo, has presented a difficult task for the prosecutors. The charges are based on the principle that, as President of Yugoslavia, Milosevic exercised command responsibility for crimes committed by institutions and forces answerable to him. Milosevic has argued that a number of the charges are false, being based on wilful misrepresentation for political reasons of events such as the alleged massacre at Racak in January 1999 and the failure of the Rambouillet discussions. He argues with regard to other charges that he either has no knowledge of them, actively sought to prevent them, or appropriately punished those responsible for criminal behaviour. The responsibility is with the prosecutors to prove the link between Milosevic and any crimes that might be proved. Thus, Richard Dicker, who is observing the case for Human Rights Watch, is of the view that: 'The prosecution has succeeded in introducing a clear base of evidence about forced displacement and murder. The more difficult part is making the link – at least in the sense of his knowledge – between Mr Milosevic himself and all those crimes.'[5]

BACKGROUND

The road to the Hague began after the defeat of Milosevic in the presidential elections in October 2000. This was followed by the defeat of Milosevic's Serbian Socialist Party in the Serbian parliamentary elections in December of that year, which very sharply raised the issue of Milosevic's future – not only as a politician, but also with regard to US and European demands that he be extradited to the Hague tribunal. This was not a simple matter to resolve, however, because a difference of position was apparent even amongst those who had been responsible for his electoral defeat, notably President Kostunica of Yugoslavia and Prime Minister Djindjic of Serbia. It had been apparent since the election of Kostunica that a delicate political balancing act existed between

Kostunica's form of moderate nationalism embodying a defence of Serb self-respect – characterized by hostility to NATO – which enabled him to defeat Milosevic in the 2000 elections, and Djindjic with his overtly pro-western reformist positions. Zoran Djindjic expressed his readiness to arrest and try Milosevic, whereas Vojislav Kostunica refused to extradite Milosevic or any other Yugoslav war crimes suspects, since extradition is outside the Yugoslav constitution. Such a step, he cautiously observed, should await reform of the legal system. Indeed, Kostunica provoked angry criticism from Djindjic for meeting with Milosevic on 13 January 2001, defending himself by asserting that: 'It is the duty of the president to communicate with leaders of political parties, in this case of the largest opposition party.'[6] Presumably, Kostunica did not wish to divide the country or alienate Milosevic's supporters more than was absolutely necessary.

Kostunica's constitutional argument against the extradition was dismissed by Momcilo Grubac, the justice minister, who argued that the constitutional ban did not apply owing to the Tribunal being a United Nations body. Other leading political figures, such as Foreign Minister Goran Svilanovic, argued instead for Milosevic to be tried in Belgrade.[7] While this discussion was taking place in January 2001, President Clinton, as one of his last executive orders, ended US economic sanctions against Yugoslavia, with the exception of about 80 Serbs, including Milosevic, his family and a number of his associates.

Tension around the issue increased in January 2001 when Kostunica met with Carla del Ponte, the chief United Nations war crimes prosecutor, during her visit to Belgrade. Arguing that a Hague trial would destabilize Yugoslavia, Kostunica again refused to extradite Milosevic and other Serbian suspects and also refused to open files in Belgrade on the whereabouts of suspected war criminals in Serbia. Kostunica reiterated his willingness to try Milosevic in Belgrade and his intention to establish a 'truth commission'. Del Ponte was angered by the refusals, and during the course of her visit Milosevic made a rare public appearance, meeting Greek Communist leader Aleka Papariga. The failure of the del Ponte visit led to a hardening of attitudes in the west, with the *International Herald Tribune* demanding: 'Even if he is not yet put on a plane to the Hague, Mr Milosevic and his indicted accomplices should be arrested.'[8]

Speaking shortly after her visit to Yugoslavia, del Ponte made the following comments:

> Belgrade will not cooperate. They told me that we have no role there. If Slobodan Milosevic is ever to be tried, it will never be in The Hague, only in Belgrade. Their explanations varied. 'The situation is dangerous.' 'Cooperation would add another element of destabilization.' 'Those prosecuted by the UN would become heroes.' 'The tribunal is in service to the United States.' 'We cannot cooperate because of NATO bombing in which Serbs were the victims.' This is a great deception on their part.[9]

> If my recent visit to Belgrade is any indication, it seems that national sovereignty is still a strong factor – it has not changed. Narrow state interests still dominate, and collective action is a problem.[10]

Further pressure was brought to bear on Kostunica in February 2001, when a delegation from the EU to Belgrade also urged him to extradite Milosevic. At this time, there was an increasing emphasis on the conditionality of aid to Kostunica's government on delivery of Milosevic to the Hague – aid which Yugoslavia badly needed. A US Congress resolution adopted in 2000 stated that Yugoslavia must demonstrate by 31 March 2001 that it was co-operating with the UN Tribunal, or it could forfeit $100 million in US aid. Belgrade continued to maintain that he would be tried in Yugoslavia for abuse of power and theft of national property. By early March, the Yugoslav Ambassador to the US, Milan Protic was assuring a congressional hearing on European security that Milosevic would definitely be arrested by the deadline – the authorities were in the process of gathering evidence to support the arrest. In fact, the Deputy Prosecutor of the UN Tribunal, Graham Blewitt, at this point indicated that it would be willing to hold part of the trial in Belgrade. He also stated that new indictments against Milosevic for war crimes in Croatia and Bosnia would also be issued, in addition to the existing indictment issued in May 1999 during the NATO attack on Yugoslavia for alleged crimes against humanity in Kosovo, including the flight in 1999 of more than 740,000 ethnic Albanians and the murder of 340 people, mostly young men, and violations of the laws and customs of war.[11]

Towards the end of March, Djindjic visited Washington to appeal for increased aid to Yugoslavia and an extension of the deadline for the arrest of Milosevic. Djindjic argued that Yugoslavia was now willing to make arrests but that a new federal law was necessary to enable it to do so legally – which would require a period of some months. Djindjic stated that Milosevic would soon be put on trial within Serbia on criminal charges and that a subsequent transfer to the Hague was not ruled out.

However, the arrest occurred sooner than might have been expected. Early on Sunday 1 April Milosevic surrendered himself after his house had been under siege for 30 hours by special forces units. Appearing before a judge, he was detained for 30 days while under investigation for abuse of office and corruption. The main charges concerned financial dealings, causing damage to the Serbian economy and bringing instability to the country during the period of hyperinflation in the early 1990s.[12]

Milosevic's lawyer Toma Fila announced that Milosevic was appealing against the detention order and asked to be allowed to defend himself as a free man. At that time, the Serbian justice minister Vladan Batic still ruled out any immediate transfer of Milosevic to the Hague, pending the passing of new legislation to make it possible. Kostunica maintained his position of opposition to extradition to the Hague, opting for the domestic trial, stating that the Hague tribunal 'practices selective justice, which is not justice at all'.[13] Kostunica also announced the creation of a presidential truth and reconciliation commission, with the aim of 'a social catharsis'.[14]

The US State Department announced on 2 April that US assistance to Yugoslavia would continue, following the arrest. However, Secretary of State Colin Powell announced that, unless Yugoslavia continued to cooperate with the Tribunal, the US would withhold support for an international donors' conference to help the Yugoslav economy. The $50 million US aid programme would continue and they would continue to support Yugoslav requests for loans from the World Bank and other institutions.

Milosevic's appeal to be released from custody pending investigation of charges, was turned down on 3 April. Milosevic, who filed his own appeal, argued that missing money had never gone into his own pockets, but had been used to pay for confidential state needs, such as the arming and financing of Serb forces in Bosnia and

Croatia, which could not have been announced in the state budget. It was considered that this statement by Milosevic would make it easier to prosecute Milosevic for war crimes in Bosnia and Croatia.

By 4 April the Tribunal had hardened its position on Milosevic's transfer to the Hague, making it an immediate demand, and the Hague tribunal formally presented the Serbian justice minister Vladan Batic with the original indictment and a warrant for Milosevic's arrest. This was at odds, however, with the position of the European Union authorities, which stated that they had no objection to Milosevic standing trial in Belgrade and coming to the Hague later. Javier Solana stated that Europe would not pressurize Belgrade to hand over Milosevic before it was ready.[15]

By June 2001, however, the pressure was mounting on Belgrade with a conference of aid donors scheduled to be held in Brussels on 29 June. On 23 June the Yugoslav cabinet decided to authorize the extradition of war crimes indictees – the legality of which was challenged by Milosevic's own lawyers. The decree formally took effect on 24 June and Milosevic's appeal was referred to the Constitutional Court. On 25 June Justice Minister Momcilo Grubac filed papers seeking Milosevic's extradition to the Hague. This step was hailed by a US official who said that, nonetheless, Washington was looking for other signs that Yugoslavia was cooperating with the Tribunal before it could decide to participate in the donors' conference, such as other indictees, and also documents sought by the Tribunal which related to alleged war crimes by Serbs.[16] The *International Herald Tribune* reported that the decision on participation was likely to come from Secretary of State Colin Powell, 'who in April had decided to extend US aid to Yugoslavia but withheld support for the donors' conference as leverage to persuade the Yugoslavs to do more'.[17]

The Serbian Socialist Party called for a demonstration against the decree and denounced the decree as unconstitutional. Party members met with Kostunica to express their concerns, but he pronounced Milosevic's extradition '"a less evil" than the country's impoverishment if foreign aid is withheld'.[18] Clearly, the leverage worked, since on 28 June Milosevic was taken by military helicopter to the NATO base in Tuzla in Bosnia and from there transported to Scheveningen prison in the Hague on 29 June. There he was due to be held in solitary confinement for the first ten days prior to an evaluation to consider the possibility of his mixing with the other

38 prisoners. At the international donors' conference on the same day, participants praised the extradition and pledged $1.28 billion in aid – slightly more than the figure of $1.25 billion that the World Bank and the European Commission had considered necessary for 2001 to commence the rebuilding process in Yugoslavia. $181.6 million was pledged from the US government.

Milosevic indicated that he would use the same Belgrade legal team that had been helping him to fight the extradition. Lawyer Branimir Gugl reported that he had received a call from Milosevic in prison, where he described his extradition as 'unconstitutional and illegal', and said that he had been kidnapped.[19] Prime Minister Djindjic defended the decision to allow the extradition, saying that any other decision would lead the country into disaster, and refused to abide by the Constitutional Court's temporary decree banning the extradition until it had further studied the matter and made a permanent ruling, saying that it was comprised of Milosevic appointees. An estimated 20,000 or more turned out to protest the extradition outside the federal parliament building in Belgrade, describing the action as treason and banditry. One of Milosevic's most high-profile western supporters, Ramsey Clark, the former US Attorney General under Lyndon Johnson, spoke at the rally, saying: 'Not in my darkest dreams could I imagine that the Serbian government can engage in a criminal act of surrendering one of their greatest citizens.'[20]

Concerns for domestic stability were caused by the resignation of the Yugoslav prime minister, the Montenegrin politician Zoran Zizic, and his Montenegrin allies in the federal government, in protest at the extradition. Kostunica's party also announced that it was breaking away from the alliance's parliamentary block in both Yugoslav and Serb parliaments, underlining the tensions that existed between Djindjic who pushed through the extradition, and Kostunica who opposed it and who, according to state news agency Tanjug, was not informed prior to the extradition. Indeed, it was widely reported that Kostunica was not even invited to the crucial meeting during the night of 27/28 June, where 15 out of 23 cabinet ministers met to discuss Milosevic's extradition. Kostunica described the Serbian government's move as 'illegal and unconstitutional', and stated that the extradition had been carried out hastily and without respect for legal procedure. This was a position that Kostunica was still maintaining in July 2002, when he reiterated his view that Milosevic should have been tried in Yugoslavia rather than the Hague.[21]

Historian and political scientist Aleksa Djilas summed up the mood of many when he said: 'We sold him for money, and we won't really get very much money for him. The United States is the natural leader of the world, but how do you lead? This just feeds the worst American instincts, reinforcing this bullying mentality.'[22] Indeed, the *International Herald Tribune* itself asked questions, referring to the Hague tribunal, that concerned many Yugoslavs at this time:

> Will this be real justice or victor's justice? No NATO commander has been indicted for the use of cluster bombs and other munitions, and no Kosovar Albanian for the killings and expulsions of Serbs from Kosovo. And how to defend a trial when the US government itself is so adamantly opposed to an international court that might one day try Americans?[23]

International condemnation of the extradition also emerged. Fidel Castro of Cuba declared that: 'The sending of Milosevic over there is illegal, it does not correspond with international laws.'[24] Russian State Duma Chair Gennady Seleznyov described it as 'undemocratic', and stated that the Hague Tribunal should instead judge NATO's supporters and allies who had bombed Yugoslavia for 78 days. President Lukashenko of Belarus also condemned the extradition. Criticism of the process, however, was forthcoming from sources other than the ones that might be expected. The Swiss daily, *Le Temps*, commented: 'It is no exaggeration to say that the extradition of the former dictator was a business deal ... Whoever the person involved – and especially if we do not like him – the law is the law, and this move was no more than an act of force at odds with principles usually upheld in the West.'[25]

THE TRIAL

On 3 July Milosevic was arraigned before the Hague court under Judge Richard May. Speaking on his own behalf, having chosen to not have counsel representation, he stated: 'I consider this tribunal a false tribunal and its indictments false indictments. It is illegal, being not appointed by the UN General Assembly. So I have no need to appoint counsel to this illegal organ.' Milosevic's key point was that: 'This trial's aim is to produce false justification for the war crimes of NATO committed in Yugoslavia.'[26]

The issue of the legality or otherwise of the extradition and the tribunal itself is much debated. The argument that both are legal is based on the notion that the ICTY is a UN body and therefore its authority supersedes that of Yugoslavia – where extradition is illegal. The illegality argument hinges on the fact the ICTY is not a properly constituted UN body. The ICTY was set up by the UN Security Council, supposedly under the provisions of Chapter VII of the UN Charter. However, Chapter VII does not give the Security Council the right to create a Tribunal or other judicial body. Thus, it is argued that 'the ICTY was created because the United States had the power to make the Security Council act in violation of the UN Charter'.[27] The UN comprises sovereign nations and, in order for a UN court to have binding authority over nations, those nations must first ratify a treaty that gives binding power to such a court. In the case of the ICTY, such a process has not occurred, leading to the argument that the ICTY derives its authority from the political and military might of its sponsors – mainly the United States but also other public and private entities – and that it is, in effect, an 'expression of Imperial power'.[28]

The first six months of the trial – up until the summer recess of August 2002 – concentrated on the charges levelled against Milosevic regarding Kosovo. Milosevic's opening statement to the court, described by the *Guardian* as 'a blistering onslaught',[29] took issue with the fundamental framework of the trial: 'This show which is supposed to take place under the guise of a trial is a crime against the Serb people and against me as head of state. It is also a crime against the truth. This is a competition between justice and injustice. The whole world knows this is a political trial.'[30] Milosevic also displayed pictures of the remains of civilian victims of the NATO bombing attacks on Yugoslavia in 1999, in the same way that the prosecutors had shown pictures of the victims of alleged Yugoslav atrocities. He also accused the prosecution team of fabrication and lying, arguing that the victims had been made into the culprits: 'Your bosses broke up Yugoslavia. They pushed Bosnia into a civil war. The Serbs did not start the war. It is nonsensical to accuse the wrong side.'[31] He also argued that the NATO intervention in 1999 had been 'concocted', because there had been no humanitarian disaster in Kosovo prior to the NATO bombing. He demanded that Clinton, Blair and other western leaders – he also accused NATO of mass murder and genocide – should be questioned about their own crimes in Kosovo and Serbia. Such high-profile witnesses may only be called, however, if their testimony directly addresses Milosevic's innocence or guilt. In fact, on 23 June 2000 the ICTY prosecutor had already declined to open an investigation into NATO's war crimes in Yugoslavia, primarily on the basis that 'the tribunal "does not have jurisdiction over crimes against peace"' – an issue also besetting the International Criminal Court, as John Laughland has observed:

> Like the Hague tribunal, the future international criminal court has postponed indefinitely any attempt to define 'crimes against peace'. Consequently, the strict circumscription of the circum- stances under which war may be waged (*ius ad bellum*) has now been replaced by an infinitely malleable series of double- standards about how it may be waged (*ius in bello*).[32]

It is also the case that the US government will not allow former Ambassador to the UN Richard Holbrooke to testify in open court at the Tribunal. A US official explained this on the basis of the need to protect intelligence sources, but the *Financial Times* newspaper took the view that it was based on 'fears that Holbrooke's appearance in open court would set a precedent for senior officials testifying before international courts ahead of the creation of the International Criminal Court, which Washington is ardently opposed to'.[33]

Referring specifically to the charges of responsibility made against him, Milosevic argued that he had given strict orders that civilians should not be harmed, and he defended the role of the army and the police, stating that they had 'defended the country coura- geously and honourably'.

During the first six months of the trial, which concentrated on the charges levelled against Milosevic with regard to Kosovo in 1999, a number of significant witnesses were called on key issues. These included Lord Ashdown on ethnic cleansing, Kosovan Albanian leader Ibrahim Rugova on Albanian aspirations in the region, former US Ambassador William Walker on Racak, Wolfgang Petritsch on Rambouillet and Rade Markovic on the expulsion of ethnic Albanians from Kosovo. On 14 and 15 March Ashdown, the former Liberal Democrat leader (who became United Nations High

Representative in Bosnia in May 2002) appeared as a prosecution witness to give an eye-witness account of one of his two fact-finding visits to Kosovo in 1998 – to the Suvo Reka Valley in Kosovo in September of that year. Ashdown reported that he had seen 16 burned-out villages and had been informed by villagers that they had been told to leave by the Yugoslav Army, who then proceeded to shell and loot the villages. In consultation with British officials, this Army action was declared in breach of the Geneva Convention and could therefore be considered a war crime. During that visit, Ashdown gave Milosevic a letter from Tony Blair telling him to stop the 'excessive and indiscriminate use of force', and at the trial said to Milosevic: 'I said to you that if you took those steps and went on doing this you would end up in this court. And here you are.'[34] In response to Ashdown's testimony, Milosevic defended the action of the Yugoslav Army on the basis that they were conducting a counter-insurgency operation against the Kosovo Liberation Army (KLA), which was a terrorist organization. Milosevic observed also that anti-terrorist operations are standard in western countries, most notably so since the conduct of the 'war against terrorism' since September 11.

Ashdown also stated that the KLA was a terrorist organization, and agreed that he had seen considerable amounts of small arms being smuggled over the border from Albania, thus strengthening Milosevic's argument with regard to the legitimacy of anti-terrorist operations by the Yugoslav Army in areas of the Kosovo country-side and villages where the KLA were operating – a key component of Milosevic's case. Indeed, Milosevic responded to Ashdown by saying: 'You are the first person sitting in this chair who does not deny that the KLA is a terrorist organisation', thus in effect agreeing that the Army's action was completely legitimate.[35]

Indeed, Ashdown appears to be an advocate of military solutions to problems. In 1999 he warned the British parliament about the Kosovo conflict, stating that there would not be a lasting and effective peace unless the west established, 'by law or in fact, an international protectorate ... Rambouillet is one way to do that, but if Milosevic will not agree we will do it anyway. The only way to do that and to secure peace is to have troops on the ground.'[36]

Ibrahim Rugova, elected as Kosovan President in March 2002, appeared as a prosecution witness in May. Rugova had been a professor of Albanian literature at Pristina University in the 1980s, and in 1989 co-founded and became president of the Democratic League of Kosovo (LDK), encouraging passive resistance to achieve republic status for Kosovo. In 1992, after holding a Kosovo-wide ballot, the LDK set up a parallel coalition government for Kosovo, with Rugova at its head. Milosevic's basic position which he attempted to draw out with Rugova was that operations were carried out by the KLA – who rejected Rugova's pacifist approach – against the Serbs of Kosovo in order to provoke the Yugoslav forces, leading to foreign intervention and the creation of a greater Albania. During cross-examination of Rugova, Milosevic attempted to establish that Rugova actually favoured Kosovo merging with Albania, into a greater Albania, against the Yugoslav constitution and breaking up its territorial integrity. Rugova, however, argued that the LDK 'aimed to have Kosovo a republic equal to the other republics in the former Federation'. In fact, in October 1991, the Albanian political parties of Kosovo, Southern Serbia, Montenegro and Macedonia had drawn up a 'Statement with Three Options', with alternative futures for Kosovo – as an independent state, as a republic within the Yugoslav federation, or as part of a Greater Albania. Although Rugova denied that the latter aim was the goal for LDK, it had actually been on the political agenda for over a decade. At the time, Albania was the only country to recognize Rugova's parallel government, as the western countries were still backing Milosevic as the guarantor of Balkan peace for supporting the Dayton Agreement and constraining the Bosnian Serbs. By 1999, when the west had changed its mind, they turned to support the KLA, making Hasim Thaci – KLA leader – chief of the Kosovan delegation at Rambouillet, superseding Rugova and the LDK. Milosevic also attempted to draw Rugova on the issue of tensions between the KLA and LDK, suggesting that Rugova had feared assassination by the KLA during the NATO bombing and saying that Rugova had gone to Milosevic asking to be protected. Milosevic said that he had arranged for Rugova to fly to Italy, but Rugova denied this and said that he had not been aware of any KLA killings. In subsequent questioning, however, Rugova did admit that some of his own party members had been killed and that they had started investigations about murders that took place after the war. A subsequent witness, under protective measure by the court and known as K6, who was a former member of Kosovo state security, testified that the KLA had indeed planned an assassination attempt against Rugova.

RACAK

A key stage in the trial has been the discussion of the alleged massacre of 45 ethnic Albanian civilians by Yugoslav forces in the Kosovan village of Racak in January 1999, which gave the immediate pretext for the NATO bombing in March 1999. The position of Milosevic on Racak is that the bodies were those of KLA combatants who had been killed in legitimate Yugoslav anti-terrorist action, following the shooting of three Yugoslav policemen, and assembled at Racak for reasons of propaganda – to stage a massacre blamed on the Yugoslav forces. To substantiate this position, Milosevic showed photographs of the bodies where no bloodstains appeared to be visible on the ground. A number of witnesses were called over this issue, including two weapons inspectors, British army officers General Karol Drewienkiewicz and Colonel Richard Ciaglinski. Drewienkiewicz was one of six deputies working for William Walker, head of the Kosovo Verification Mission (KVM) – set up in October 1998 under the control of the OSCE – and Ciaglinski worked with him. They were responsible for liaison with the Yugoslav authorities, meeting on an almost daily basis with the Serbian Cooperation Commission. Following the battle in January between the Yugoslav forces and the KLA, Drewienkiewicz and William Walker visited the site. Drewienkiewicz observed that, although the corpses were lying close together and shot in the neck, he was unable to find any bullet cartridges nearby. He also explained to the court:

> We were, I think, very, very conscious that you can sometimes make a situation worse by overreacting to an initial report. And there had been instances of that in December of 1998 when alarming reports came in which, upon investigation, were less awful than the first report – that many times atrocities would turn out not to be the fault of those originally suspected.

As an example, Drewienkiewicz told the court how he had been 'traveling in a KVM/Yugoslav Army convoy that had been fired on, resulting in the wounding of two of his own inspectors. At first he thought it was warning fire from Serbian forces, but after an investigation the KLA admitted to the attack.'[37]

In fact, a report was published early in 2002 by a team of Finnish pathologists which would seem to give some support to Milosevic's position on Racak. Dr Helena Ranta stated in a German TV broadcast that she was 'conscious that one could say that the whole scene in the small valley was arranged ... This conclusion was included in our first investigation report, and also in our later forensic investigations, which we made in November 1999 directly in Racak'.[38] In fact, Drewienkiewicz's statement that the corpses were shot in the neck was not borne out by the Finnish pathologists' report, which stated that most of the corpses 'were covered by multiple wounds from different angles and elevations, characteristic of a firefight rather than a close range execution. Only one had been shot at close range and no signs of post-mortem mutilations were found. The team could not confirm that the victims were from Racak.'[39]

When William Walker himself testified before the court, he stated that he had seen the bodies of mostly elderly men lying in pools of blood from bullet wounds. Milosevic, when cross-examining him – having alleged that Walker had supported the Contras when working for the US government in central America and still worked for the CIA – displayed photographs of the scene at Racak and asked him if he saw blood in the picture. 'No, not in this picture', Walker replied. It was Milosevic's contention that this supported the argument that the scene was fabricated.[40]

Milosevic also challenged the independence of elements within the Kosovo Verification Mission, alleging that they favoured the ethnic Albanians and gathered information for NATO intelligence purposes. To support these accusations, he quoted the Italian inspectors, who criticized 'Walker and his British chief of operation, Karol John Drewienkiewicz for rejecting any cooperation with Serb authorities', seeing the KVM as 'controlling the mission's information flow, and most serious of all, for using the mission to make contacts with UCK rebels and train them to guide NATO to targets in the subsequent bombing'.[41] Ciaglinski denied that he had been a spy for NATO, but Pascal Neuver, a Swiss verifier stated that 'We understood from the beginning that the information gathered by the KVM was used for completing the information gathered by NATO satellites. We had the impression we were gathering intelligence for NATO.'[42]

Drewienkiewicz also made an interesting statement with regard to the alleged planned, forcible expulsion of ethnic Albanians from Kosovo as stated in the indictment against Milosevic:

My opinion was that up until the moment we drove out of Kosovo on the 20th of March, I came across no indications that there was a plan to expel the civilian population. I was absolutely clear that there was a plan to deal with the KLA which would involve bringing in reinforcements of the Yugoslav Army and those reinforcements had started to arrive before we left. But I was not – I saw no evidence that such a plan to expel the civilian population existed as at 20th March.[43]

RAMBOUILLET

Wolfgang Petritsch took the stand to suggest that Milosevic had rejected the opportunity for a peaceful settlement of the Kosovo issue at the Rambouillet negotiations. The Austrian diplomat Petritsch was the European Union envoy for Kosovo at the height of the conflict and led the EU delegation at the Rambouillet peace talks in February 1999. Petritsch argued that the peace talks had ended on a positive note and that, although the Serbs had not signed it, he was fairly confident that they would sign after consultations with Milosevic. However, he observed that the international negotiating team had noticed a change in attitude from the Serbs towards the Rambouillet accord from February to March 1999. This change he ascribed to Milosevic, stating that he had wilfully turned down the accord after which the NATO bombing began on 24 March and thus was responsible for the war. Milosevic's position was that the Rambouillet accords were an ultimatum explicitly allowing the occupation of the whole of Yugoslavia by NATO forces and therefore unacceptable to a sovereign state. The part of the Treaty to which Milosevic objected was Appendix B, section 8, which stated:

> NATO personnel shall enjoy, together with their vehicles, vessels, aircraft, and equipment, free and unrestricted passage and unimpeded access throughout the FRY including associated airspace and territorial waters. This shall include, but not be limited to, the right of bivouac, maneuver, billet and utilization of any areas or facilities as required for support, training and operations.[44]

It is hard to imagine any head of state agreeing to the occupation of their country and it seems likely that the US government was aware of this, intentionally – according to one senior State Department official – creating a situation where Yugoslavia would be forced into war.[45]

AN 'INSIDER' WITNESS

Former head of the Department of State Security of the Serbian Ministry of the Interior, Rade Markovic, called as a prosecution witness, testified that Milosevic did not engineer a campaign to drive out ethnic Albanians from Kosovo, and was not responsible for any war crimes in the province. He informed the court that Milosevic had received daily briefings about police and army operations against ethnic Albanians during the conflict, but stated that he had acted in accordance with the law. He also stated that Milosevic had ordered that no atrocities be carried out against ethnic Albanian civilians and that: 'Specifically, there was this ban on which you [Mr Milosevic] insisted ... that houses in Kosovo must not be set on fire and nothing must be stolen.'[46] Markovic also informed the court that 200 interior ministry troops were prosecuted for crimes, and around the same number from the Yugoslav Army. This was a very significant statement in relation to Milosevic's 'command responsibility', around which much of the prosecution case hinges, for it indicates that army policy, for which Milosevic was ultimately responsible, was to punish those guilty of crimes. Markovic also agreed with Milosevic's position that ethnic Albanians had fled Kosovo because of NATO bombs rather than because of persecution by the Serbs. On 26 July, Markovic testified that he had been held in gaol in Belgrade for the previous 17 months and that he had been tortured during that time to force him to agree to give false testimony.[47] As Markovic had been called as a prosecution witness, there was some expectation that as a high-ranking member of Milosevic's former circle, he would be able to strongly reinforce the prosecution case. However, that has clearly not been the case, and as the court broke for four weeks summer recess many observers considered that Milosevic had made a rigorous and convincing case against the charges levelled against him, and that the prosecution had faced many setbacks in their attempts to establish the veracity of the indictments with regard to Kosovo.

Notes

INTRODUCTION

1. S.L.Woodward, *Balkan Tragedy. Chaos and Dissolution after the Cold War*, Washington, D.C., 1995, p.7.
2. Ibid.
3. D. Chandler, *Bosnia. Faking Democracy after Dayton*, London, 2000.
4. N. Malcolm, *Bosnia: A Short History*, New York, 1994.
5. N. Malcolm, *Kosovo: A Short History*, New York, 1998.
6. Woodward, *Balkan Tragedy*, p.7.
7. J.B. Allcock, *Explaining Yugoslavia: Modernisation in the 19th and 20th Centuries*, London, 1998.
8. M. Glenny, *The Balkans: Nationalism, War and the Great Powers, 1804–1999*, London, 1999.

CHAPTER 1

1. J. Rothschild, *East Central Europe between the Two World Wars*, Seattle and London, 1974, p.204.
2. M. Crnobrnja, *The Yugoslav Drama*, London and New York, 1994, p.40.
3. Ibid., p.42.
4. F. Singleton, *Twentieth Century Yugoslavia*, London and Basingstoke, 1976, pp.49–50.
5. Ibid., p.50.
6. Crnobrnja, *Yugoslav Drama*, p.43.
7. T. Judah, *The Serbs. History, Myth and the Destruction of Yugoslavia*, New Haven and London, 1997, p.97.
8. Ibid., p.99.
9. Ibid., p.101.
10. L. Benson, *Yugoslavia. A Concise History*, Basingstoke, 2001, p.23.
11. F. Singleton and B. Carter, *The Economy of Yugoslavia*, London and Canberra, 1982, p.51.
12. Ibid., p.60.
13. Ibid., p.63.
14. Ibid., p.64.
15. V. Dedijer, quoted in Singleton and Carter, *Economy of Yugoslavia*, p.65.
16. J.R. Lampe, *Yugoslavia as History. Twice There was a Country*, Cambridge, 2002, p.181.
17. Rothschild, *East Central Europe*, p.275.
18. Singleton and Carter, *Economy of Yugoslavia*, p.65.
19. Rothschild, *East Central Europe*, p.275.
20. Ibid., p.269.
21. Ibid., p.210.
22. Singleton and Carter, *Economy of Yugoslavia*, p.82.
23. Ibid., p.91.

24. D.H. Aldcroft and S. Morewood, *Economic Change in Eastern Europe Since 1918*, Aldershot, 1995, p.68.
25. Ibid., pp.66–7.
26. Crnobrnja, *Yugoslav Drama*, p.54.
27. Rothschild, *East Central Europe*, p.216.
28. Ibid.
29. Benson, *A Concise History*, p.49.
30. Ibid.
31. Rothschild, *East Central Europe*, p.213.
32. Crnobrnja, *Yugoslav Drama*, p.62.
33. Ibid., p.59.
34. Ibid.
35. Ibid., pp.59–60.
36. Benson, *A Concise History*, p.54.
37. Crnobrnja, *Yugoslav Drama*, p.60.
38. Benson, *A Concise History*, p.59.
39. S.L. Woodward, *Balkan Tragedy. Chaos and Dissolution after the Cold War*, Washington, D.C., 1995, p.24.
40. Crnobrnja, *Yugoslav Drama*, p.63.

CHAPTER 2

1. F. Singleton and B. Carter, *The Economy of Yugoslavia*, London and Canberra, 1982, p.95.
2. F. Singleton, *Twentieth Century Yugoslavia*, London and Basingstoke, 1976, p.86.
3. S.L. Woodward, *Balkan Tragedy. Chaos and Dissolution after the Cold War*, Washington, D.C., 1995, p.24.
4. L. Benson, *Yugoslavia. A Concise History*, Basingstoke, 2001, p.70.
5. Ibid., p.66.
6. J. Rothschild, *East Central Europe between the Two World Wars*, Seattle and London, 1974, p.264.
7. Quoted in J.R. Lampe, *Yugoslavia as History. Twice There was a Country*, Cambridge, 2002, p.199.
8. Singleton, *Twentieth Century Yugoslavia*, p.83.
9. P. Auty, *Tito. A Biography*, Harmondsworth, 1980, p.194.
10. Ibid., p.200.
11. Lampe, *Yugoslavia as History*, p.205.
12. Ibid., p.207.
13. Singleton, *Twentieth Century Yugoslavia*, p.88.
14. Lampe, *Yugoslavia as History*, p.208.
15. T. Judah, *The Serbs. History, Myth and the Destruction of Yugoslavia*, New Haven and London, 1997, p.117.
16. Ibid., p.128.
17. Lampe, *Yugoslavia as History*, p.206.
18. Auty, *Tito*, p.21.
19. Lampe, *Yugoslavia as History*, p.207.
20. Quoted in Auty, *Tito*, p.206.
21. Judah, *The Serbs*, p.120.

22. Lampe, *Yugoslavia as History*, p.207.
23. Singleton, *Twentieth Century Yugoslavia*, p.86.
24. Ibid., p.93.
25. Ibid., p.94.
26. V. Dedijer, *Tito Speaks. His Self-portrait and Struggle with Stalin*, London, 1954, p.158.
27. Benson, *A Concise History*, p.75.
28. Dedijer, *Tito Speaks*, p.186.
29. Auty, *Tito*, p.238.
30. Singleton, *Twentieth Century Yugoslavia*, p.95.
31. Ibid., p.99, note 24.
32. Dedijer, *Tito Speaks*, p.205.
33. Ibid., p.206.
34. Ibid.
35. Ibid., p.223.
36. Auty, *Tito*, p.284.
37. Ibid., p.211.
38. Singleton and Carter, *Economy of Yugoslavia*, p.93.
39. Quoted in ibid., p.95.
40. Ibid., p.94.

CHAPTER 3

1. S.L. Woodward, *Balkan Tragedy. Chaos and Dissolution after the Cold War*, Washington, D.C., 1995, p.25.
2. F. Singleton, *Twentieth Century Yugoslavia*, London and Basingstoke, 1976, p.105.
3. F. Singleton and B. Carter, *The Economy of Yugoslavia*, London and Canberra, 1982, p.99.
4. Ibid.
5. Ibid., p.101.
6. W.S. Churchill, *The Second World War, Volume 6, The Triumph and the Tragedy*, London, 1956, pp.194–5.
7. A.B. Ulam, *Expansion and Coexistence. Soviet Foreign Policy 1917–73*, Second Edition, New York, 1974.
8. Singleton, *Twentieth Century Yugoslavia*, p.112.
9. Ibid., p.120.
10. Singleton and Carter, *Economy of Yugoslavia*, pp.124–5.
11. Singleton, *Twentieth Century Yugoslavia*, p.144.
12. Ibid., p.176.
13. Woodward, *Balkan Tragedy*, p.26.
14. Singleton, *Twentieth Century Yugoslavia*, p.177.
15. Woodward, *Balkan Tragedy*, pp.27–8.
16. H. Poulton, *The Balkans. Minorities and States in Conflict*, London, 1991, p.5.
17. Singleton, *Twentieth Century Yugoslavia*, p.139.
18. Ibid., p.270.
19. Ibid., p.272.
20. Ibid.

21. M. Crnobrnja, *The Yugoslav Drama*, London and New York, 1994, p.75.
22. S.P. Ramet, *Balkan Babel. The Disintegration of Yugoslavia from the Death of Tito to the Fall of Milosevic*, Fourth Edition, Boulder, Colorado, 2002, p.8.
23. Poulton, *The Balkans*, p.6.
24. Crnobrnja, *Yugoslav Drama*, p.73.
25. Quoted in Singleton, *Twentieth Century Yugoslavia*, p.282.

CHAPTER 4

1. S.L.Woodward, *Balkan Tragedy. Chaos and Dissolution after the Cold War*, Washington, D.C., 1995, p.45.
2. R.J. Crampton, *Eastern Europe in the Twentieth Century*, London and New York, 1994, p.386.
3. M. Chossudovsky in M. Spencer (ed.), *The Lessons of Yugoslavia*, Toronto, 2000, p.166.
4. M. Spencer in M. Spencer (ed.), *The Lessons of Yugoslavia*, p.11.
5. S. Flounders, *The Bosnian Tragedy*, International Action Center, USA, 1995.
6. M. Chossudovsky in Spencer (ed.), *The Lessons of Yugoslavia*, p.167.
7. F. Singleton and B. Carter, *The Economy of Yugoslavia*, London and Canberra, 1982, p.250.
8. D.H. Aldcroft and S. Morewood, *Economic Change in Eastern Europe Since 1918*, Aldershot, 1995, p.170.
9. Woodward, *Balkan Tragedy*, p.49.
10. Ibid.
11. I. Bicanic in O. Sjoberg and M.L. Wyzan (eds), *Economic Change in the Balkan States: Albania, Bulgaria, Romania and Yugoslavia*, London, 1991, p.27.
12. M. Crnobrnja, *The Yugoslav Drama*, London and New York, 1994, p.85.
13. Woodward, *Balkan Tragedy*, p.52.
14. Ibid., p.58.
15. I. Bicanic in Sjoberg and Wyzan (eds), *Economic Change*, p.29.
16. M. Chossudovsky in Spencer (ed.), *The Lessons of Yugoslavia*, pp.169–70.
17. Woodward, *Balkan Tragedy*, p.57.
18. Ibid., p.61.
19. L. Benson, *Yugoslavia. A Concise History*, Basingstoke, 2001, p.135.
20. Woodward, *Balkan Tragedy*, p.65.
21. H. Poulton, *The Balkans. Minorities and States in Conflict*, London, 1991, p.57.
22. Ibid., p.59.
23. Benson, *A Concise History*, p.137.
24. Poulton, *The Balkans*, p.60.
25. Ibid.
26. Ibid., p.61.
27. Ibid., p.65.
28. Ibid., p.66.
29. Ibid.
30. Crnobrnja, *Yugoslav Drama*, p.93.

31. Interview with Norah Beloff in 'Yugoslavia: The Avoidable War', film produced by George Bogdanich and Martin Lettmayer, 2000.
32. Benson, *A Concise History*, p.146.
33. Crnobrnja, *Yugoslav Drama*, p.94.
34. R. Thomas, *Serbia under Milosevic. Politics in the 1990s*, London, 1999, p.48.
35. W. Zimmerman, 'The Last Ambassador' in *Foreign Affairs*, vol.74, no.2, pp.4–5.
36. L. Sell, *Slobodan Milosevic and the Destruction of Yugoslavia*, Durham and London, 2002, p.173.
37. Zimmerman in *Foreign Affairs*, vol.74, no.2, p.8.
38. Ibid.
39. Woodward, *Balkan Tragedy*, p.90.
40. Thomas, *Serbia under Milosevic*, p.47.
41. Ibid., p.9.
42. Speech by S. Milosevic, 28 June 1989.
43. Thomas, *Serbia under Milosevic*, p.43.

CHAPTER 5

1. N. Beloff, *Yugoslavia. An Avoidable War*, London, 1997, p.25.
2. M. Crnobrnja, *The Yugoslav Drama*, London and New York, 1994, p.109.
3. J. Seroka in J. Seroka and V. Pavlovic (eds), *The Tragedy of Yugoslavia. The Failure of Democratic Transformation*, New York and London, 1993, p.78.
4. Crnobrnja, *Yugoslav Drama*, p.112.
5. S.L.Woodward, *Balkan Tragedy. Chaos and Dissolution after the Cold War*, Washington, D.C., 1995, p.115.
6. Crnobrnja, *Yugoslav Drama*, p.113.
7. L. Benson, *Yugoslavia. A Concise History*, Basingstoke, 2001, p.139.
8. W. Zimmerman 'The Last Ambassador' in *Foreign Affairs*, vol.74, no.2, p.8.
9. Woodward, *Balkan Tragedy*, p.117.
10. Seroka in Seroka and Pavlovic (eds), *Tragedy of Yugoslavia*, p.81.
11. Crnobrnja, *Yugoslav Drama*, p.145.
12. Ibid.
13. J.R. Lampe, *Yugoslavia as History. Twice There was a Country*, Cambridge, 2002, p.360.
14. Seroka in Seroka and Pavlovic (eds), *Tragedy of Yugoslavia*, p.81.
15. Woodward, *Balkan Tragedy*, p.123.
16. Ibid.
17. Ibid., p.132.
18. Crnobrnja, *Yugoslav Drama*, p.149.
19. Zimmerman in *Foreign Affairs*, vol.74, no.2, pp.6 and 17.
20. Crnobrnja, *Yugoslav Drama*, p.152.
21. R. East and J. Pontin, *Revolution and Change in Central and Eastern Europe*, Revised Edition, London, 1997, p.250.
22. Crnobrnja, *Yugoslav Drama*, p.153.
23. Woodward, *Balkan Tragedy*, p.157.
24. Ibid., p.158.

25. Beloff, *An Avoidable War*, pp.23–4.
26. Lampe, *Yugoslavia as History*, p.369.
27. Woodward, *Balkan Tragedy*, p.136.
28. Beloff, *An Avoidable War*, p.27.
29. Benson, *A Concise History*, p.159.

CHAPTER 6

1. A. Burgess, *Divided Europe. The New Domination of the East*, London, 1997, p.137.
2. Interviewed in 'Yugoslavia: The Avoidable War', film.
3. M. Glenny, *The Balkans 1804–1999. Nationalism, War and the Great Powers*, London, 1999, p.637.
4. S.L. Woodward, *Balkan Tragedy. Chaos and Dissolution after the Cold War*, Washington, D.C., 1995, p.165.
5. Quoted in T. Judah, *The Serbs. History, Myth and the Destruction of Yugoslavia*, New Haven and London, 1997, p.173.
6. Ibid.
7. Woodward, *Balkan Tragedy*, p.149.
8. Interviewed in 'Yugoslavia: The Avoidable War', film.
9. Interviewed in ibid.
10. Interviewed in ibid.
11. Interviewed in ibid.
12. M. Glenny, *The Fall of Yugoslavia. The Third Balkan War*, London, 1996, p.112.
13. G. Swain and N. Swain, *Eastern Europe since 1945*, Basingstoke and London, 1998, p.198.
14. Woodward, *Balkan Tragedy*, p.137.
15. M. Crnobrnja, *The Yugoslav Drama*, London and New York, 1994, p.166.
16. Ibid.
17. Ibid., p.167.
18. Ibid., p.169.
19. R. Thomas, *Serbia under Milosevic. Politics in the 1990s*, London, 1999, pp.99–100.
20. Quoted in Judah, *The Serbs*, p.179.
21. L. Silber and A. Little, *The Death of Yugoslavia*, Revised Edition, London, 1996, p.174.
22. M. Almond, *Europe's Backyard War. The War in the Balkans*, London, 1994, p.211.
23. 'Yugoslavia: The Avoidable War', film.
24. Burgess, *Divided Europe*, p.138.
25. Silber and Little, *Death of Yugoslavia*, p.185.
26. Ibid., p.186.
27. Judah, *The Serbs*, p.189.
28. Quoted in Silber and Little, *Death of Yugoslavia*, pp.186–7.
29. Almond, *Europe's Backyard War*, p.212.
30. Crnobrnja, *Yugoslav Drama*, p.192.
31. Ibid., p.193.
32. Ibid., p.194.

33. Woodward, *Balkan Tragedy*, p.169.
34. Almond, *Europe's Backyard War*, p.227.
35. Crnobrnja, *Yugoslav Drama*, p.199.
36. Almond, *Europe's Backyard War*, p.226.
37. L. Benson, *Yugoslavia. A Concise History*, Basingstoke, 2001, p.164.
38. Woodward, *Balkan Tragedy*, p.147.
39. Ibid.
40. Interviewed in 'Yugoslavia: The Avoidable War', film.
41. Interviewed in ibid.
42. Interviewed in ibid.

CHAPTER 7

1. S.L. Woodward, *Balkan Tragedy. Chaos and Dissolution after the Cold War*, Washington, D.C., 1995, p.197.
2. S.P. Ramet, *Balkan Babel. The Disintegration of Yugoslavia from the Death of Tito to the Fall of Milosevic*, Fourth Edition, Boulder, Colorado, 2002, p.204.
3. Ibid., p.203.
4. W. Zimmerman, 'The Last Ambassador' in *Foreign Affairs*, vol.74, no.2, p.9.
5. W. Pfaff, 'Invitation to War' in *Foreign Affairs*, vol.72, no.3, p.103.
6. Poulton, *The Balkans. Minorities and States in Conflict*, London, 1991, p.41.
7. R. East and J. Pontin, *Revolution and Change in Central and Eastern Europe*, Revised Edition, London, 1997, p.266.
8. Poulton, *The Balkans*, p.42.
9. Quoted in ibid., p.42.
10. N. Beloff, *Yugoslavia. An Avoidable War*, London, 1997, p.35.
11. Ibid.
12. Poulton, *The Balkans*, p.44.
13. 'Yugoslavia: The Avoidable War', film.
14. Ramet, *Balkan Babel*, p.207.
15. Woodward, *Balkan Tragedy*, p.193.
16. Beloff, *An Avoidable War*, p.97.
17. Woodward, *Balkan Tragedy*, p.194.
18. Interviewed in 'Yugoslavia: The Avoidable War', film.
19. Woodward, *Balkan Tragedy*, p.283.
20. 'Yugoslavia: The Avoidable War', film.
21. *New Left Review*, 17, Sept/Oct 2002.
22. Woodward, *Balkan Tragedy*, p.197.
23. Ibid., p.283.
24. Ramet, *Balkan Babel*, p.206.
25. C.G. Boyd, 'Making Peace with the Guilty' in *Foreign Affairs*, vol.74, no.5, p.25.
26. M. Glenny, *The Balkans: Nationalism, War and the Great Powers, 1804–1999*, London, 1999, p.639.
27. Ramet, *Balkan Babel*, p.208.
28. 'Yugoslavia: The Avoidable War', film.
29. Ibid.

30. M. Parenti, *To Kill a Nation. The Attack on Yugoslavia*, London, 2000, p.74.
31. Ibid., pp.74–5.
32. Ibid., p.75.
33. Boyd in *Foreign Affairs*, vol.74, no.5, p.28.
34. 'Yugoslavia: The Avoidable War', film.
35. Boyd in *Foreign Affairs*, vol.74, no.5, p.23.
36. 'Yugoslavia: The Avoidable War', film.
37. Parenti, *To Kill a Nation*, p.52.
38. Ramet, *Balkan Babel*, p.213.
39. Ibid., p.217.
40. Ibid., p.224.
41. Ibid., p.232.
42. East and Pontin, *Revolution and Change*, p.272.
43. 'Yugoslavia: The Avoidable War', film.
44. East and Pontin, *Revolution and Change*, p.274.
45. D. Chandler, *Bosnia. Faking Democracy after Dayton*, London, 2000, p.1.
46. *Guardian*, G2 section, 11 October 2002, p.3.
47. M. Chossudovsky in M. Spencer (ed.), *The Lessons of Yugoslavia*, Toronto, 2000, p.172.
48. Ibid.

CHAPTER 8

1. W.K. Clark, *Waging Modern War. Bosnia, Kosovo and the Future of Combat*, New York, 2001, p.418.
2. P.W. Rodman, 'The Fallout from Kosovo', in *Foreign Affairs*, vol.78, no.4, p.46.
3. T. Judah in M. Waller, K. Drezov and B. Gokay (eds), *Kosovo. The Politics of Delusion*, London, 2001, p.21.
4. Ibid.
5. J. Pettifer in Waller, Drezov and Gokay (eds), *Kosovo*, p.26.
6. Quoted in I.H. Daalder and M.E. O'Hanlon, *Winning Ugly. NATO's War to Save Kosovo*, Washington, 2000, p.10.
7. 'Yugoslavia: The Avoidable War', film.
8. Ibid.
9. Pettifer in Waller, Drezov and Gokay (eds), *Kosovo*, p.28.
10. 'Yugoslavia: The Avoidable War', film.
11. M. Parenti, *To Kill a Nation. The Attack on Yugoslavia*, London, 2000, p.99.
12. Quoted in ibid., p.99.
13. 'Yugoslavia: The Avoidable War', film.
14. Parenti, *To Kill a Nation*, p.103.
15. 'Yugoslavia: The Avoidable War', film.
16. Judah in Waller, Drezov and Gokay (eds), *Kosovo*, p.23.
17. Pettifer in Waller, Drezov and Gokay (eds), *Kosovo*, p.28.
18. The Rambouillet Accords, February 1999.
19. Foreign Affairs Committee, Fourth Report, *Kosovo*, Vol.1, 23 May 2000.
20. M. Littman QC, *Neither Legal nor Moral. How NATO's war against Yugoslavia breached international law*, London, 2000, p.10.
21. Quoted in Parenti, *To Kill a Nation*, p.113.

22. Adam LeBor, *Milosevic. A Biography*, London, 2002.
23. Littman, *Neither Legal nor Moral*, p.3.
24. Speech by Alice Mahon MP.
25. Littman, *Neither Legal nor Moral*, p.8.
26. Ibid., p.15.
27. Quoted in Parenti, *To Kill a Nation*, p.111.
28. Quoted in ibid., p.110.
29. *Labour Focus on Eastern Europe*, 64/1999, p.25.
30. Waller, Drezov and Gokay (eds), *Kosovo*, p.vii.
31. FT.com, 29 March 1999.
32. *Sunday Herald*, 5 April 1999.
33. *International Herald Tribune*, 10 January 2001.
34. Ibid., 6/7 January 2001.
35. 'Humanitarian Situation in the Federal Republic of Yugoslavia and the Activities of the Yugoslav Red Cross', Yugoslav Red Cross Report, Belgrade, February 2000.
36. D. Johnstone, *Collective Guilt and Collective Innocence*, <www.emperors-clothes.com>.
37. Foreign Affairs Committee Report.
38. Daalder and O'Hanlon, *Winning Ugly*, p.205.
39. C. Jacobsen in M. Spencer (ed.), *The Lessons of Yugoslavia*, Toronto, 2000, p.327.
40. *International Herald Tribune*, 18 October 1999.
41. UNHCR/OSCE Report, 'Assessment of the Situation of Ethnic Minorities in Kosovo', November 1999–January 2000, p.1.
42. Ibid.
43. Foreign Affairs Committee, Fourth Report, *Government Policy Towards the Federal Republic of Yugoslavia and the Wider Region Following the Fall of Milosevic*, 20 March 2001, p.xxxvi.
44. International Committee of the Red Cross, Emergency Appeal 2000, Federal Republic of Yugoslavia.
45. UNHCR/OSCE Report, p.14.
46. *Labour Focus on Eastern Europe*, 64/1999, pp.44–5.
47. UNHCR/OSCE Report, p.5.

CHAPTER 9

1. *Guardian*, 1 January 2002.
2. R. Thomas, *Serbia under Milosevic. Politics in the 1990s*, London, 1999, p.422.
3. Ibid., p.424.
4. Ibid., p.422.
5. Ibid., p.426.
6. Ibid., p.257.
7. Adam LeBor, *Milosevic. A Biography*, London, 2002, p.259.
8. Ibid.
9. Ibid., p.264.
10. Thomas, *Serbia under Milosevic*, pp.265–6.
11. Quoted in Thomas, *Serbia under Milosevic*, p.327.

12. BBC News Online, 25 September 2000.
13. 'In a Spin', 11 October 2000, <www.zmag.org/johnstonem.htm>.
14. *International Herald Tribune*, 13 December 2000.
15. Ibid.
16. Ibid.
17. Radio Free Europe/Radio Liberty, *Balkan Report*, vol.4, no.81, 31 October 2000.
18. Beta Newsagency, Belgrade, 26 September 2000, <www.emperors-clothes.com>.
19. From UPI Report, quoted in <www.stopnato.org.uk> 27 September 2000.
20. Ibid.
21. From Serbian News Network, 23 October 2000, <www.antic.org.SNN>.
22. BETA Daily News, 10 October 2000, <www.beta-press.com>.
23. Ibid.
24. *Financial Times*, 26 March 2002.
25. Ibid.
26. *International Herald Tribune*, 26 December 2000.
27. Ibid.
28. Ibid, 3/4 February 2001.
29. Ibid.

CHAPTER 10

1. *Guardian*, 12 February 2002.
2. *Los Angeles Times*, 12 February 2002.
3. *Observer*, 3 March 2002.
4. Ibid.
5. *Guardian*, 27 July 2002.
6. *Financial Times*, 15 January 2001.
7. *International Herald Tribune*, 17 January 2001.
8. Ibid., 27/28 January 2001.
9. Ibid., 1 February 2001.
10. Ibid.
11. *International Herald Tribune*, 8 March 2001, 6 April 2001, 30/6–1/7 2001.
12. Ibid., 2 April 2001.
13. Ibid., 4 April 2002.
14. Ibid.
15. Ibid.
16. Ibid., 26 June 2001.
17. Ibid.
18. Ibid.
19. Ibid., 30/6–1/7 2001.
20. Ibid.
21. Agence France Presse, 26 July 2002.
22. Ibid.
23. Ibid.
24. Workers World News Service, 12 July 2001.
25. Quoted in WSWS, 4 July 2001 by Chris Marsden and Barry Grey.
26. WWNS, 12 July 2001.

27. CAMPEACE statement, June 2001.
28. Ibid.
29. *Guardian*, 15 February 2002.
30. Ibid.
31. Ibid.
32. *Guardian*, 16 February 2002.
33. Agence France Presse, 12 June 2002.
34. WSWS, 27 March 2002.
35. *Guardian*, 16 March 2002.
36. WSWS, 27 March 2002.
37. WSWS, 8 May 2002.
38. WSWS, 2 May 2002.
39. WSWS, 20 July 2002.
40. Associated Press, 12 June 2002.
41. Ibid.
42. Ibid.
43. Ibid.
44. The Rambouillet Accords.
45. WWNS, 18 July 2002.
46. Agence France Presse, 26 July 2002.
47. <www.emperors-clothes.com>, 27 July 2002.

Index

Compiled by Sue Carlton

Financial Times 149, 164
Finn, Peter 150
First World War 9–10, 12–15
Foreign Operations Appropriations
    Law 101–513 (1991) 57
France 14, 16, 26, 91, 113, 120
Franco, Francisco 24
Frankfurter Allgemeine Zeitung 91
Franz Ferdinand, Archduke 12
free market economy 2, 61, 66, 73,
    83, 131, 138, 140, 148

GATT 49
Geneva Peace Conference (1992)
    114
genocide 68, 154
    see also ethnic cleansing
Genscher, Hans-Dietrich 89
German Secret Service (BND) 91–2,
    125
Germany 9, 26–8
    Albanian *Gastarbeiter* 125
    arms to Croatia 92
    and break-up of Yugoslavia 2, 56,
        87, 88, 89, 91–2, 152–3
    invasion of Yugoslavia 1941 25,
        27, 29
    raw materials from Yugoslavia
        16–17, 26–7
    recognition of Slovenia and
        Croatia 75, 88, 89, 92, 100,
        101, 112
    support for Croatia 94, 113
    trade with Yugoslavia 16–17, 18
Glenny, Misha 3–4, 89, 92, 114
Gligorov, Kiro 80
Gorazde 120
Gorbachev, Mikhail 56, 152
Gospic 96
Gowan, Peter 131, 137
Greater Albania 109, 127, 139, 150,
    166
Greater Serbia 2, 74, 150
Greece 28, 43, 44, 82, 101
Grubac, Momcilo 157, 160
Guardian 163
Gugl, Branimir 161

Haavisto, Pekka 133
Hackworth, David C. 92

Hague tribunal 117, 138, 156, 157,
    158, 159, 160, 162
    see also International Criminal
        Tribunal for the Former
        Yugoslavia (ICTY); Milosevic,
        Slobodan, trial of
Helsinki Final Act (1975) 86
Herzeg-Bosna 111
Hitler, Adolf 16, 26, 27
Holbrooke, Richard 125, 126, 164
Human Rights Watch 156
Hungarian Arrow Cross 30
Hungarian Socialist Party 81
Hungarians 50–1, 65
Hungary 8, 10, 28, 29, 45, 91, 114
    communist parties 82
    NATO membership 123
Hurd, Douglas 89

I-FOR 121
Illyrian movement 10
IMF 39, 112, 121
    conditionality 2, 40, 59, 148, 152
    reform programme 57–8, 59,
        61–2, 63, 69, 71, 73, 83
India 49
Interim National Legislature (INL)
    19
Internal Macedonian Revolutionary
    Organization (IMRO) 80, 81
International Committee of the Red
    Cross 117, 136–7
International Committee to Defend
    Slobodan Milosevic 155
International Criminal Court (ICC)
    164
International Criminal Tribunal for
    the Former Yugoslavia (ICTY)
    132, 154, 163–4
    see also Hague tribunal
International Herald Tribune 136,
    144–5, 150, 157, 160
international law 124, 129–30,
    162–4
Iran 107, 108, 118
irredentism 82, 101, 149, 153
'Islamic Declaration, The' 107
Italy 16, 26, 27, 28, 29, 31, 35
Ivanov, Igor 147